ANTIHEROES

Books by Ilan Stavans in English

Fiction
The One-Handed Pianist and Other Stories

Non-Fiction
Art & Anger: Essays on Politics and the Imagination

Bandido: Oscar 'Zeta' Acosta & the Chicano Experience

The Hispanic Condition:
Reflections on Culture and Identity in America

Imagining Columbus: The Literary Voyage

Editor
Tropical Synagogues:
Short Stories by Jewish Latin American Writers

Growing Up Latino: Memoirs and Stories
(coedited with Harold Augenbraum)

Translation
Sentimental Songs, by Felipe Alfau

ANTIHEROES

Mexico and Its Detective Novel

Ilan Stavans

Translated from the Spanish by
Jesse H. Lytle and Jennifer A. Mattson

With a Foreword by Donald A. Yates
and an Epilogue by Hiber Conteris

Madison ● Teaneck
Fairleigh Dickinson University Press
London: Associated University Presses

Associated University Presses
440 Forsgate Drive
Cranbury, NJ 08512

Associated University Presses
16 Barter Street
London WC1A 2AH, England

Associated University Presses
P.O. Box 338, Port Credit
Mississauga, Ontario
Canada L5G 4L8

The paper used in this publication meets the requirements
of the American National Standard for Permanence of Paper
for Printed Library Materials Z39.48–1984.

Library of Congress Cataloging-in-Publication Data

Stavans, Ilan.
  [Antihéroes. English]
  Antiheroes : Mexico and its detective novel / Ilan Stavans ;
translated from the Spanish by Jesse H. Lytle and Jennifer A.
Mattson ; with a foreword by Donald A. Yates and an epilogue by
Hiber Conteris.
    p. cm.
  Includes bibliographical references and index.
  ISBN 0-8386-3644-6 (alk. paper)
  1. Detective and mystery stories, Mexican—History and criticism.
2. Mexican fiction—20th century—History and criticism. I. Lytle,
Jesse H. II. Mattson, Jennifer A. III. Title.
PQ7207.D48S83   1997
863'.087209972—dc20   96-27657
                                                          CIP

As I reexamine my past life, the opposite of what happens to Hercule Poirot happens to me: I see in the shadow of the past a forest of unresolved cases.

—Jorge Ibargüengoitia, *Autopsias rápidas*

All happy families are more or less dissimilar; all unhappy ones are more or less alike, says a great Russian writer at the beginning of a famous novel (*Anna Arkadievitch Karenina,* transfigured into English by R. G. Stonelower, Mount Tabor Ltd., 1880). The pronouncement has little if any relation to the story to be unfolded now, a family chronicle, the first part of which is, perhaps, closer to another Tolstoi work, *Detstvo i Otrochestvo* (*Childhood and Fatherland,* Pontious Press, 1858).

—Vladimir Nabokov, *Ada or Ardor*

Contents

8 CONTENTS

Foreword

THE development of detective fiction away from its time-honored classical forms and traditions toward the condition of what might be termed "mainline" writing is a significant feature of the history of popular literature in the second half of our century. In Latin America, where the detective story has always been an imported type of literary expression, this same phenomenon can be observed.

Some forty years ago, I began a study of detective fiction as it had been produced in Spanish America, focusing mainly on Argentina and Mexico, the two nations where it had been most extensively cultivated. By 1960 I was able to discern and describe what I termed the "humanization" of the detective story in Argentina. Authors such as Manuel Peyrou, María Angélica Bosco, and Marco Denevi, I suggested, were involved in this process. At that time, I did not observe the same phenomenon occurring with Mexican detective fiction writers, who almost uniformly were writing novels and short stories clearly imitative of (mainly) long-established North American and English models.

But more than three decades have passed since then and the situation—predictably—has changed. For this reason, it is a great boon to have Ilan Stavans's carefully and intelligently researched, up-to-date study of Mexican detective literature. He has provided us with an examination of the genre's prehistory, its imitative period and, perhaps most importantly, brings us beyond the mere loosening of the detective story's traditional restrictions (which I termed "humanization") to an appreciation of the narrative innovations that have been applied to crime fiction in Mexico in the wake of the celebrated literary "boom" in Latin American letters. He signals the tumultuous year of 1968 as a watershed year—certainly a valid observation—and amply justifies his case.

In the space of the quarter century that has passed since that year, Spanish American detective literature in general has developed and matured and has begun to attract attention abroad. Spanish-language detective novels and short stories in translation have appeared in many countries, in none more frequently than in the U.S., where a new audience can today read the work of Argentines Manuel Peyrou, Marco Denevi, Jorge Luis Borges, and his long-time collaborator Adolfo Bioy Casares, as well as that of Ricardo Piglia, whose *Artificial Respiration* takes the genre to a new frontier.

From Mexico, too, have come novels that can now be read in English. Carlos Fuentes's *The Hydra Head*, which is his version of the first adventure of the Mexican secret service, was translated immediately into half a dozen languages. Moreover, we now have rendered into English the first five Mexican private eye detective narratives written by Paco Ignacio Taibo II, whose work Ilan Stavans discusses here at length. Another recent and singular development in the field is the appearance in 1992 of Lucha Corpi's novel, *Eulogy for a Brown Angel,* in which we read of the first adventure of Gloria Damasco, a Chicana feminist detective. These are surely signs of the genre's coming of age in Mexico.

When I see the names of the authors and critics whom Stavans has chosen to discuss individually in his second chapter, particularly those who contributed to Mexico's "Golden Age" of detective fiction (the forties and fifties), I am reminded of my first trip to Mexico City in 1958 to study Mexican detective literature, when I met many of these people. Antonio Helú, in a real sense the father of the Mexican detective story, was cordial, helpful, and hospitable to a fault. For the better part of a month I was incorporated into his literary *tertulia* at a bar in downtown Mexico City, not far from the Alameda. The conversations of those long afternoons taught me many things about writers and writing.

María Elvira Bermúdez also became a friend on that trip, and we kept up a lively correspondence for many years. A *licenciada* working with the Mexican Supreme Court, she was one of Mexico's first modern-day feminists, and opened up many social issues that had not previously been explored from the woman's point of view. Through her I met and interviewed her son-in-law, Carlos Monsiváis, one of the earliest literary critics to deal with detective fiction.

Doubtlessly the first and undeniably the most distinguished of Mexican men of letters to reveal his admiration for the detective story was the author, essayist, and humanist, Alfonso Reyes, with whom I spent a memorable afternoon at his extraordinary library-residence on Benjamin Hill Street in the capital. I had told María Elvira that I would like very much to meet him; she led me there the next day. Reyes was to live only a few more months, but his enthusiasm for detective literature was as fresh and vital as that of a young person who had just discovered the charms of the genre. Years later I found a page of his where he declared that a person's youth comes to an end and old age sets in at the moment when he loses his love for detective stories. We talked that afternoon for barely an hour. He said he felt ill and showed signs of physical weariness, but he insisted on showing me his library and then giving me a sampling of his books, which he patiently signed and inscribed.

It was in another piece that Reyes paid his highest compliment to the detective story. It appeared in a book of essays published in Mexico in 1945 and has been quoted many times since. He wrote: "Built-in plot interest and coherence in the action! What more did Aristotle require? The detective story is the classical literary genre of our time."

It is the contributions of these and other Mexican writers that form the textual basis for Ilan Stavans's study. I take great satisfaction in seeing their work now receiving the careful critical attention that they merit.

Finally, we should point out that, thanks to Ilan Stavans, we now have a clear and comprehensive illustration of how this imported literary form and its conventions can be modified to accommodate the cultural perspective and social attitudes of a single country— a particularly fascinating phenomenon. In short, I recommend this insightful documentary to all readers, especially to those who have been proclaiming for years that the detective story has been "written out," has reached a dead end. Ilan Stavans, a true believer, has demonstrated from his own perspective that this simply is not true. Edgar Allan Poe invented the form in April 1841. More than a century and a half later, the genre is alive and well, adapting and evolving. What else to say but—*Viva el género policial!*

DONALD A. YATES

Introduction

WHY do people read detective and espionage novels so avidly? Why is this writing so attractive to the public's collective imagination? These questions are difficult, but not unanswerable. In comparison with so-called "serious" literature that demands patience and concentration, these books represent a pleasant break or alternative. They neither have nor aspire to have any educational or transformative pretensions. They are written for consumption and entertainment, or at least leave that impression. If we follow them through their historical journey, short compared with other literary genres, like the psychological, the lyrical, or the epic, we still find they have traveled incalculable miles. The masters are Wilkie Collins, Agatha Christie, Georges Simenon. The works of Friedrich Dürrenmatt, Borges, and perhaps Kafka, those of Alain Robbe-Grillet and the *nouveau roman,* Umberto Eco's two encyclopedic novels, Vladimir Nabokov's stylized works, and various pieces from Italo Calvino are all detective experiments. From these, one can deduce that during the twentieth century this type of literature, admittedly popular, has attracted authors whose aesthetic affiliations run in distinct directions, who, upon exercising their pens, have widened the scope of the genre and even redefined it.

In pedagogical and critical terms, academic circles still demonstrate a bias against the more traditional, commonplace detective novels. However, interest in the experimental side has been growing steadily, as well as in its English heritage. In addition, this attraction to, for instance, Kafka's *The Process,* Borges's "Death and the Compass," or Nabokov's *Pale Fire,* has curiously prompted the critic to devote energy to the study of the history of the detective novel as an entity and a sum of its parts, from Edgar Allan Poe, Charles Dickens, and Collins to Raymond Chandler and Dashiell Hammett, including Agatha Christie and Ross MacDonald.

This implies that the writers are teaching the critics not to blindly dismiss this fountain of creativity upon which we feed daily, whether through text or adaptations for television and cinema. Such an impact prompts analysis of the genre's metabolism, commercial appeal, occasionally prosaic language, narrative tools, and

13

finally, its conventions. Critics of distinct persuasions, among them Tzvetan Todorov, Edmund Wilson, Dennis Porter, Umberto Eco himself, Jacques Lacan, Geoffrey Hartman, Stephen Knight, Michael Holquist, Roger Caillois, and Roland Barthes, have approached the detective novel in search of a missing facet of sophisticated art: Marxists, for example, believe that in its manifestation lies an authentic expression of the soul of the people; semiotics, in turn, have approached them with an analysis of their treatment of the delay of information, which becomes suspense; linguists come to them hoping to find the language of the streets, the syntax of the lower class; the Russian formalists, whose labor culminated in Roman Jakobson and Boris Tomashevsky, understand that the history of literature isn't the mere succession of masterpieces but what he calls "literality—the dialogue between genres.[1] To varying degrees, all of these approximations are appreciable in that they are closing the cavernous gap that has long separated literature "worthy of academic attention" from the rest, those which indulge the public.

But there are those who take an opposing stance. In 1983, Glenn W. Most and William W. Stowe, in their anthology *The Poetics of Murder,* argued that if the Golden Age of detective writing had reached its sunset, then so had the critic, who had not progressed comparably in analyzing this type of literature. They claim that important approximations had arisen before World War II, and what we hear now is merely an echo.[2] If this argument—which, in any form, denounces this delay when one considers the date of the first nineteenth-century detective contributions of Poe, Vidocq, Hugo, Dostoevsky, and Dickens—is valid, then what occurred in the last fifty years has been a democratizing and egalitarian phenomenon: the detective novel has been reborn around the world with new fervor, from Spain to Czechoslovakia, from Israel to Latin America. Although in the early decades of this century there was already an atmosphere of ersatz—i.e., imitative and emulative manifestations of Dorothy L. Sayers, Agatha Christie, Arthur Conan Doyle, or the hard-boiled American that flourished boundlessly—the creation of a unique, unmistakable identity, an idiosyncratic detective who, in his personae, represents Havana, Prague, or Tel Aviv, has been only a recent development.

The balance of writing over the past few years has presented us with explorations of that theme in Argentina, Cuba, Chile, and Mexico. Authors like Borges, Manuel Peyrou, Mempo Giardinelli, Mario Vargas Llosa, Rubem Fonseca, Gabriel García Márquez, Ernesto Sábato, Manuel Puig, Vicente Leñero, Adolfo Bioy Casares, just to name a few, have prompted the critics to condescend to analyze their roots in detective literature, the literary wellspring of which they have partaken. The anthologies of Borges and Adolfo Bioy Casares, Rodolfo J. Walsh, Juan Jacobo Bajarlía, and Donald A. Yates have propagated material of impressive quality. The academic works of Yates, Antonio Panells, and Amelia S. Simpson, among others, have explained how, when, and by what means the first Latin American attempts at detective fiction arose.

The majority, however, are panoramic works; they discuss a work or an author and are hesitant to penetrate deeply into a single national context. Furthermore, there are studies by Andreu Martín, Manuel Vázquez Montalbán, Juan Madrid, Eduardo Mendoza, and other practitioners in the Iberian peninsula. In *The Spanish Sleuth*,[3] Patricia Hart compiled a series of interviews and critical essays that make this narrative current in the post-Franco age more accessible. In the case of Mexico, there are two anthologies and various scattered articles, one of them from Carlos Monsiváis. But, as in other Latin American countries, there is yet to arrive a complete examination explaining the bonds among Mexican texts, detailing influences, the nuances of context, and the impact of the world's detective writing upon Mexico itself. That, precisely, is my objective in this study.

From Yates to Monsiváis, seldom has the motive force behind this genre's analysis removed it from the category of "parody;" the truth is that no other classification has been sufficiently convincing. When all is said and done, the creation of a detective text in Spanish is always an imitative task. It was in the United States, Great Britain, and France where the genre was cultivated, not in the Spanish-speaking world. Thus it is impossible to read, for example, "Approach to Almotasim" without remembering Chesterton; Rubem Fonseca's *A Grande Arte* (High Art) or Paco Ignacio Taibo II's *Cosa fácil* (An Easy Thing), without invoking Chandler's pedestrian, agitated, and "dirty" language from *The Big Sleep*.

Part 1 examines the status of the Mexican novel after the so-called *La Onda*, or "The Wave," movement and, using works from José Agustín, Gustavo Sáinz, and Carlos Fuentes as a springboard, offers an analysis of the Distrito Federal as an ad hoc backdrop for native detective literature. Starting with Bakhtin's concepts of "parody" and "stylistic parody," it will then construct an observation point from which one can feasibly study the Mexican thriller.

Translators' note: Titles are translated into English and placed in parenthesis only when a translation is already available. The translation is used thereafter.

From Mexico's conquest as a colony, through the independence and revolutionary periods, up to present day, part 2 analyzes the development of the police and the state. This will be followed by a commentary on the real investigators and actual cases that have captured public imagination. It then covers the "Golden Age" of the detective novel in the forties and fifties, from a realistic angle, with examples from Antonio Helú, José Martínez de la Vega, and María Elvira Bermúdez. Equal attention is paid to the works of Rafael Ramírez Heredia and Paco Ignacio Taibo II, the latter having given the thriller its own unique personality and made it commercially viable outside Mexico. Along with Monsiváis, the critical forum is studied, where Xavier Villaurrutia, Jorge Ibargüengoitia, and especially Alfonso Reyes have confessed their affinity for these "escapist" novels and relentlessly argue their pros and cons. I then discuss the contributions, creative or critical, of Jorge Luis Borges, Eduardo Mendoza, and Julio Cortázar and how they influenced the Mexican contingent of authors, compared with those of other Spanish-speaking countries.

I mentioned before that the objective of this work is to study the development and presence of detective literature in Mexico. I should add here that I did not exclusively focus my attention on novels and short stories that subscribe to the formula; in part 3 I analyze how some of the traditional or "classical" elements have been scattered about and are hidden, explicit behind other masks, or on occasion more "sophisticated."

In the Latin American spectrum, Mexico can be compared to Argentina as a promoter and producer of detective fiction; what distinguishes the two countries is that the former lacks a figure of Borges's stature who has revolutionized the boundaries of tradition on a global scale. Carlos Fuentes, the most renowned Mexican writer, has made his own mark with *La cabeza de la hidra* (The Hydra Head), an espionage novel. However, it is a work of minor importance in his personal corpus, and, for that matter, in the entire detective genre, which includes the likes of John LeCarré and Ian Fleming. Aside from certain celebrated translations of the English, French, Italian, and German from a few writers who frequent the genre, especially Taibo II, it was the 1963 Biblioteca Breve Prize from Seix-Barral in Barcelona, awarded to Vicente Leñero's *Los albañiles,* and the critical acclaim that met Ibargüengoitia's *Las muertas* (The Dead Girls) that marked the peak of foreign interest in Mexican detective literature. The implication is that this literary activity continues to be a local exercise, as it has always been in the United States—although, certainly, in New

York, Los Angeles, or Miami, that which is "local" is always injected with a strong dose of worldliness.

These are some of the themes that unfold in the course of the following pages, which, even if devoid of suspense, are faithful disciples to the elegant art of tying up loose ends, an art immortalized by Sam Spade, Sherlock Holmes, and Erik Lönnrot.

Addendum to the American Edition

THE landscape of detective fiction in and from Mexico has dramatically changed since *Antihéroes: México y su novela policial* first appeared in Spanish. For one, Paco Ignacio Taibo II has been acclaimed as one of Latin America's most original and attractive voices. His novels are now available in almost all European languages. A new generation of writers and critics is taking shape, thanks to periodicals like *Crimen y Castigo,* a Mexico City-based Pan American magazine devoted to thrillers and what Taibo II calls *lo neopolicial.* Also, as I interpret it, the extensive and enthusiastic reception granted to my book, both north and south of the Rio Grande, is a sign of its solid, ongoing invigoration, not only in my native country but in Latin America as a whole. Some examples: *Review,* a biannual magazine published by the Americas Society in New York City, has published a special issue devoted to thrillers in the region; the English translations of Rubem Fonseca's dirty-realist novels, and of Ricardo Piglia's *Respiracion artificial* (Artificial Respiration, Duke University Press, 1994), which, like its precursor Rodolfo Walsh's *Operación Masacre,* builds an astonishing bridge between thrillers, metafiction, and historical reflection, have enjoyed considerable critical attention. And the critical torch has also moved onward: a number of doctoral dissertations on the subject have been completed since 1992, and Jorge Hernández Martín, at Dartmouth College, has published *Readers and Labyrinths: Detective Fiction in Borges, Bustos Domecq, and Eco* (Garland, 1995) and has begun a serious critical exploration of Taibo II's fictional universe. Hernández Martín is only one of the many young scholars devoting their attention to the subject.

My analysis ends in 1990 and, aside from listing English translations and including a useful interview with Taibo II, I have not added any further segments, nor have I expanded the bibliography. I wish to thank Walter Cummins and Harry Keyishian for inviting me to guest edit a special issue of *The Literary Review* (Fall 1994) and for soon after finding ways to make this American edition come to life. My gratitude to the staff of the New York Public

Library, Mexico's Hemeroteca Nacional, and Columbia University's Butler Library, as well as to Taibo II, José Emilio Pacheco, Donald A. Yates, and Hiber Conteris for their friendship. The latter two were kind to write an introduction and epilogue in English, and to offer their unrestricted openness to answer my questions.

ANTIHEROES

Part 1

1

Point of Departure

THE year 1968 was critical in Mexico's history, replete with political tumult and agitation. On 13 August, some 150,000 protesting students marched to the Zócalo in the Distrito Federal. Less than a month later, on 1 September, housewives and office workers joined the fracas in a rally totaling more than 300,000 people. Just before the lighting of the Olympic torch, the government of Gustavo Díaz Ordaz, hoping to project a more tranquil, reliable image of a country hungry for foreign investments, perpetrated a brutal military massacre of civilians. The site, the Plaza de las Tres Culturas de Tlatelolco. The impact resounded through every level of Mexican society. A new social conscience began to evolve; the lack of national democracy and the dictatorial supremacy of the Partido Revolucionario Institucional (P.R.I.), which had been in power since 1929, became clear and unmistakable.

At a literary level, the voice of repression and dissidence became increasingly louder, utilizing a variety of narrative techniques. From Elena Poniatowska's journalistic account *La noche de Tlatelolco* (Massacre in Mexico), published by Era three years after the incident, to Fernando del Paso's *Palinuro de México* (Palinuro of Mexico), whose first edition was released by Joaquín Mortiz in 1980, a multitude of novels, theatrical productions, and short stories sprang up, interpreting the incident from social, historical, psychological, and anthropological points of view. "It was an instinctive repetition that assumed the form of a ritual of atonement; the correspondences with the Mexican past, especially with the Aztec world, are fascinating, scary, and repulsive. The killings of Tlatelolco reveal to us that a past that we believed was buried is still alive and erupts around us," said Octavio Paz.[1]

Before 1968, the nation's literature had already expressed refreshing, adolescent dreams and obsessions. A new generation was emerging with a unique vision of the world, one that drew inspiration from Allen Ginsberg, William Burroughs, and North American

25

beats. Writers born after 1940, among them *l'enfant terrible* José Agustín, author of novels such as *La tumba* and *De perfil,* and Gustavo Sainz, creator of *Gazapo,* which had appeared just a few years earlier, were penetrating the narrative genre and set the standards for a new ideological and cultural direction. Their art glorified counterculture, drugs, the opposition enraged by the establishment, and alternative understandings. They undertook social protest with irreverent language and an open, defiant sexuality.[2] The movement was later labeled *la Onda,* "the Wave," and its repercussions were felt for years to come. Among la Onda's many innovations, its members demanded the recognition of Mexico City, the already monstrous metropolis, as a place of passion and mystery, a labyrinth of mirrors and alleys, and especially as a superficies, beneath which people maneuver through secret redoubts and channels, invisible to the superficial observer. With prosaic adventures of youth gone astray, they accurately stressed that, at a comparative level, the province lacked reality and perversion, fascinations that only the Distrito Federal could offer. In the maelstrom of bestial instincts, transitivity, and conglomeration of humors and people, there was an unparalleled attraction that forged the entire artistic impetus of the era.

The attempt to place the capital at the center of the literary scene, however, significantly preceded Agustín and Sáinz, although from other perspectives. Sigüenza y Góngora, and Sor Juana,[3] among other colonial writers, had already produced texts which discussed the city's architecture, plagues, longstanding regimes, and the planning of its aqueducts and sewers. But neither they nor the novels of the revolution or from the *Contemporáneos* had applied the proper cosmetics to cast the metropolis as a lone and supreme protagonist.

Only upon the arrival of Carlos Fuentes' *La región más transparente* (Where the Air is Clear) in 1958, a book whose fragmented structure was inspired by futurism, resembled the works of John Dos Passos, and whose ambitious task was to integrate all social strata *à la* Balzac, did the Distrito Federal acquire its own narrative force. Although Fuentes set the majority of his action between 1951 and 1954, the text interprets all forty years following the revolution. The web of avenues, the metropolitan passions, the bars and their lawlessness, the corruption, the Francophile aristocracy, political ambition: everything revolves around a common hub, Ixca Cienfuegos, which bonds and amalgamates the literary mare magnum. Beginning with an epigraph from Alexander von Humboldt, the nineteenth-century German scientist, labeling the city as "*la región más transparente del aire"*—later Alfonso Reyes versified the same epigraph in *Visión de Anáhuac*—the author's most outstanding accomplishment was to make the capital not just the focus of attention but a vivacious creature, like Joyce did with Dublin, Émile Zola or Eugenio Sué with Paris, and Benito Pérez Galdós with Madrid. The effect is an imposing collage, a mosaic of juxtaposed yearning, initiation rites, power confrontations, and amorous relationships.

La Onda sets sail with the contributions of Fuentes, but its objective is to portray a less complacent, more juvenile and wild side of the urban area. Agustín's first novel in 1964, recounted by its narrator, Gabriel, is a description of the sexual pleasures, linguistic offenses, and unsettling exploits of a group of kids, children of the capital's rich families. *De perfil* continues on this tack, although it has a more ambitious, testimonial, and satirical tone, the product of a more mature author. The young protagonist is seen from all angles: beside his brother, with his family, in school, and in philosophical discussions. In its colloquial, grammatically disdainful text, we visit the urban underworld, reminiscent of *Gazapo,* a novel of seduction which, with its characters Menelao and Rosita in search of liberty and better outlets for personal expression, is the Mexican response to Jack Kerouac's *On the Road.*

From 1958 to the present, the capital is the essential theme, the keystone of the Mexican novel. It appears in the works of Arturo Azuela, Luis Spota, José Emilio Pacheco, Luis Zapata, and has made multiple appearances in those of Carlos Fuentes.[4] Intentions change, there are diverse facets; the city is seen as an anti-utopia, as a vehicle of nostalgia, or as a dangerous, ensnaring spider web. Or it is a zoo of aberrations in miniature, where at any moment one may discover obsolete, monstrous entities, ignominious and violent beings.

In addition to recasting the Distrito Federal as a literary theater, we owe another contribution to la Onda. In *The Mexican Novel (1967–1982),* John Brushwood studies Mexico's literary path from *El periquillo sarniento* (The Itching Parrot) by "the Mexican Thinker" José Joaquín Fernández de Lizardi, to the recent fin de siécle production. He asserts that the primordial characteristic of the country's writing in the seventies and eighties is the metafictitious device, or the observation of a certain creative act by its ·own author; Salvador Elizondo is obviously of great import to this aesthetic trend. Brushwood adds that books abound whose purpose, once the killings at Tlatelolco incited a change in social conscience, have been to portray the unstable personality of the

metropolitan. Furthermore he notes, that a return to the old literary style in Mexico, such as it was before 1947, began with the
publication of Agustín Yáñez's *Al filo del agua* (At the Edge of the
Storm), and culminated with Juan Rulfo's *Pedro Páramo* in 1955.[5]
Brushwood adds two more outstanding characteristics: one is the
mixture of certain techniques of the testimonial and chronicle
genre with those of fiction; the other is the proliferation of female
voices, among them María Luisa Puga, Elena Poniatowska, and
Angeles Mastretta.

But truth is even more expansive. By the end of la Onda, new
creative doors, formerly reserved solely for mass media, were
opened for Mexican writers. Suddenly there was an exquisite selection of subgenres at their disposal, like espionage, science fiction, melodrama, and the thriller, just to name the most popular.
To become submerged in these latitudes, properties of an imported
popular culture, meant to fully recognize their lineages so their
attributes could be adapted to the immediate reality. The awaken-
ing of this "subsidized culture," as Ibargüengoitia called it, was,
without doubt, one of the vestiges left by la Onda, one which at
the onset antagonized the status quo and later consented to play
by the rules, only then to metamorphose collective reality from
the inside.

There are countless novels that use borrowed structures. Some
examples: Fuentes' *Cristóbal Nonato* (Christopher Unborn) is a
parody of Orwell's 1984 and Aldous Huxley's *Brave New World;*
Hugo Hiriart's *Galaor* was inspired by medieval sagas and the
fables of fantastical lands, like J. R. R. Tolkien's *Lord of the Rings*
or *The Narnia Chronicles* by C. S. Lewis; Julio Cortázar, although
Argentine, published his ingenious Fantomas contra las empresas
multinacionales in Mexico in comic format. But the principal affection, that which attracted the most interest, was toward the thriller
and tales of espionage. Innumerable novels evolve around a crime
or contain confidential information, novels where there are spies,
private eyes, logical deductions, or conspiracies that threaten the
security of an individual or even all of society. From Sergio Pitol's
El desfile del amor to Vicente Leñero's *Asesinato,* and including
The Hydra Head) and other recent works from Paco Ignacio Taibo
II, it would not be an exaggeration to claim that consciously or
not, the detective genre has captivated the Mexican writer, and
that Mexico City, with its perquisites and joys, is almost always
host to the crimes and getaways. The detective novel in Mexico,
then, is the daughter of la Onda: an illegitimate and bastard daugh-

ter, one must admit, because, as the reader shall see, the true father is in London, New York, or Paris.

This claim, however, is only half true, and it is the duty of this work to prove it. The reader shall realize in the following pages that investigators out of the Sherlock Holmes mold have been in Mexico since the forties, and that, with some fluctuation, their presence in the narrative panorama is yet to be eclipsed. They are almost always placed in the Distrito Federal, in poor sectors or among the aristocrats. What affiliation, then, what link does this literary current have with la Onda? Thanks to Agustín and Sáinz, among others, a revitalizing spirit has helped this type of novel flourish, but without the inferiority complex that it had suffered previously. The detectives, formerly upper-class conservatives or miserable but fascinating crooks, by the seventies did not fear clashes among social classes or groups, nor did they dissimulate their violence when confronting criminality. They were drinkers, womanizers, smokers, or even drug addicts, but without appearing any worse off for it. They openly ridiculed the corrupt government and political travesty. In other words, detectives have a long history, but la Onda bestowed previously unknown mettle and gallantry upon them. Moreover, the public, barraged by television and cinematic thrillers, was able to recognize and identify with Mexican detectives. Why? Because la Onda had demonstrated that the distinction between "serious" and "popular" culture is only in the observer, and that both should be recognized and appreciated. Although it is not until the arrival of Paco Ignacio Taibo II that the city acquired a life of its own, it must be recognized that in the works of José Martínez de la Vega and Rodolfo Usigli it was already becoming an entity with its own, singular character. This forces us to consider the Mexican detective novel as a precursor to such "urban-centrism." Before *Where the Air Is Clear,* there were already narrative models aspiring to treat the Distrito Federal as a literary character.

The benefits of the detective formula are many and can assimilate into diverse methods and objectives. Mere entertainment, without any greater glory or aspiration, is quite feasible. Or, if one starts with a crime, it is possible to recreate a precarious human situation, describe a deceptive, sordid atmosphere, undertake a historical analysis, or explore an identity. As will be explained, detective fiction in Mexico includes each and every one of these possibilities. Within this context, the contributions of detective fiction before and after 1968 must be examined. To accomplish this, it is necessary to understand the complicated mechanism of adaptation through which a writer may introduce and play with a subgenre. To imitate a foreign model implies a parody, thus this term and its connotations must be understood. First and foremost, the following questions must be answered: When did the detective genre penetrate Mexico? Who read these works and in what language? Who wrote the first native attempts? How did they copy the model and what elements did they introduce to differentiate their work? Who came next? Is there a "Mexican" contribution to detective fiction?

2

Parody and the Police

He decided to anticipate the vanity awaiting all man's efforts;
he set himself to an undertaking which was exceedingly complex and, from the very beginning, futile. He dedicated his scru-
ples and his sleepless nights to repeating an already extant book
. . . Menard (perhaps without wanting to) has enriched, by
means of a new technique, the halting and rudimentary art of
reading: this new technique is that of the deliberate anachronism and the erroneous attribution.

Jorge Luis Borges, "Pierre Menard, Author of the *Quixote*"

THIS tale of an apocryphal French symbolist who attempted not
to copy, but rather to rewrite *Don Quixote* is perhaps the most
representative example of a modern parody: a writer starts with a
preexisting work, adapts it to his time, and makes the reader see
it in a fresh and innovating way. The creation of actual, uncon-
strained literature is quite similar to this type of self-reflexive, imitative exercise. But what exactly is parody?

According to the *Princeton Encyclopedia of Poetry and Poetics,*[1]
parody is a literary mechanism as old as poetry. Pages 600 and 601
of the 1965 edition advise that, to begin with, one must differentiate
between comic parody and literary, or critical, parody. The former
is based on mockery, ridicules stereotypes, and ties the sacred to
the profane in an attempt to provoke a catharsis through laughter.
But it is the latter that is pertinent here; it is a parody through
which one text exaggeratedly imitates another, or even an entire
genre. Perhaps better than anyone else, Mikhail Bakhtin, the Russian critic who focused his work on the epic novel, Freud, Kafka,
Dostoevsky, and narrative polyphony, elaborated a hypothesis
about this category that combined both comic and literary parodies. This analysis appears in "From the Prehistory of Novelistic
Discourse" a segment from one of his major works, *The Dialogic
Imagination.*[2]

31

According to Bakhtin, parody (or travesty) is a seed in whose germ the embryo of the modern novel gestated. Its origins can be traced to Greco-Hellenistic drama, which laid the groundwork for the rise of novelistic art, inasmuch as it liberated the word from the powers of myth and fostered a distance between reality and language, which would prove indispensable for the birth of the realist novel. The Russian critic details his embryonic metaphor in a level that is impossible to examine here. But it is clear that its manifestations were realized within the framework of popular festivals and settings permitted by the state and/or church, which prompted its acceptance within the framework of the law. In its attempt to desecrate the divine by injecting it with laughter, parody enabled human language to satirize sacred existence. Once this was realized, the next step was to make fun of the surrounding media, now owing no deference toward the religious sphere. In this way, parody served as a safety valve—the pivot point that allowed the transition from acts of sacrament and medieval liturgic song to the Renaissance novel.

The aforementioned implies a mechanism of "renovation," of "reorganization;" a religious text opens itself to disrespectful or self-reflexive commentary from outside. To understand this phenomenon of superimposition, occasionally irreverent, Bakhtin examines the idea of the social hybrid.

For the parody to be an artistic alternative, the writer should be aware of a surrounding cultural duality, of a certain "hybridization." This occurs when reality is affected by two or more cultural models, which promotes two ideological appreciations. Thus, the parody is an attempt to offer words "with intentional quotation marks," at once outside and within its own context. These indirect words come about in a hybrid composed of two styles or two "languages" that merge or even cross: the parodied language (that of an epic poem, for instance) and that which parodies it.

A useful and illuminating example is *Don Quixote:* Cervantes first had to assimilate the rules, structures, and literary suppositions of chivalric novels. In addition, he had to understand the pseudo-epic language that *Tirant lo Blanc* or *Amadís de Gaula* used, the metabolism of the picaresque novel, and the lyrical novel itself, which he practiced, not to mention lyrical genres. But it all would have been unnecessary if the Spaniard had lived in another historical setting, one foreign to the baroque cultural spirit in Spain (1580–1700), closely associated with the Counter-Reformation, which was heavily inclined to mock medieval pedantry. In effect, the representation of reality in baroque works, from Torcuato

Tasso's *Jerusalem Liberated* to the plays of Calderón de la Barca, accents the theatrical nature of life, relying on oxymorons and asyndetons, attempts at literary imitation, and the ability to mutate things. Without this "hybridization" which stresses opposites— essence and appearance, light and shadow, dream and conscious- ness, life and death, etc.—Cervantes would not have achieved the depth and character of the nobleman and his servant.

This parodical exercise was made possible by the saturation of chivalric novels and the heritage of the picaresque novel, which had reached paroxysm between 1605 and 1615, and also by the duality and reigning existential pessimism at that literary moment. The proof is that, despite Cervantes's ability to play with those literary traditions through a satirical language, the seventeenth- century reader was able to identify them without any difficulty. That is Bakhtin's explanation in "Forms of Time and of the Chrono- tope in the Novel," also from *The Dialogic Imagination*. He affirms that Don Quixote has an enormous significance in literary history because, through the phenomenon of hybridization, he bestows upon his two characters metaphorical, allegorical significance.[3] Maurice Keen supports this opinion in his interpretive history of chivalry, where he describes the novel's apotheosis in the age of Cervantes and how the author, via the parody, took advantage of the centuries of saturation which kept the caballeros and their damas alive in the popular imagination:

> More important than any of this, however, were changes which, in the sixteenth century, were taking place at a deeper level, and were altering the shape of the social and political structures in which chivalry had in the past flourished. What we see at the end of the middle ages is in consequence not so much the decline of chivalry, but the alteration of its appearance—which is, indeed, rather what Cervantes's indulgence in his Don Quixote, his appreciation of the grandeurs of chivalry as well as its follies, might lead us to expect. The forces that in the medie- val past had given it life and impetus were still at work, but the outward aspects in which they found expression were changing, and the old name was losing its appositeness.[4]

Parody, then, is far from being a "pure" genre (while the tragedy and the epic are, according to Bakhtin). To the contrary, according to his own typology, parody is carnivalesque, in that it devours, decomposes, and juxtaposes some, only to build others.

It must be added that Bakhtin, in *Problems of Dostoevsky's Poet- ics*,[5] discusses a crucial concept, "generic memory." He argues that every piece of literature, upon its emergence, not only participates in the historical moment in which it is born, but also bears the distinctive elements of the genre's tradition, and in this way forms a part of the global history of that tradition. Thus every work implicitly carries with it every past, present, and future work that subscribes to the same literary genre.

In "Discourse in the Novel," also in *The Dialogic Imagination*,[6] the Russian critic offers other valuable concepts: that of "stylization," for example, which is the representation that one language makes of another (meaning an idiomatic, not structural, parody); that of "variation," which is the adaptation of a piece from one time to another without altering its message, psychology, or dynamic; and likewise that of the "parodical stylization," which is the satirization or destruction of a genre and its language via parodical mechanisms. These three concepts revolve around the same phenomenon. Each one, however, refers to a different level of assimilation and accommodation and limits itself respectively to the linguistic dimension, varying certain details, or undertaking a more complete transformation.

Bakhtin's role in Russian literary critique during the first decades of the century is fundamental in that it supplants the European, western logocentric vision, which idolized Tolstoy and the monologic novel, and put Dostoevsky, the carnival, and dialogic narrations in the picture. With his contribution, the bourgeois novel could accept a genealogy that was broader, more ludic, more assimilative, where, along with Richardson, Fielding, Stendhal, and Flaubert, one would have to include Diderot, Lawrence Sterne, and Cervantes. Its reach, then, is based upon moving marginal, peripheral narrative to the exclusive site that until then had been occupied by the realist heritage.

"Carnaval / Antropofagia / Parodia," a 1979 essay by the Uruguayan critic Emir Rodríguez Monegal,[7] explains the difficulties and applicability of Bakhtin's theories to literary studies of Latin America and discusses the works of, among others, Severo Sarduy in the Castillian sphere and Harold de Campos in Brazil. His contribution consists of examining, from the arrival of Hernán Cortés at Tenochtitlán in 1519, up to the Boom of the sixties and seventies, how the adaptation of the native culture to foreign standards meant, obviously, an infinite chain of works that were imitative and laudatory of foreign models. The phenomenon of carnivalization and parody of European or North American literary trends permeated every vanguard, from Sor Juana Inés de La Cruz and her celebration of Góngora's cultism, to Mario Vargas Llosa and Gabriel García Márquez and their seeming apprenticeship under

Hemingway and Faulkner, not to mention Leopoldo Lugones, Herrera y Reissig, drawn to the Count of Lautrémont.

From discovery in 1492 to independence in 1824, these two terms, "carnivalization" and "parody," are essential to understanding the cultural mechanisms within Latin America. First and foremost, the mixture of races and the colonial intentions of making the New World an economic, political, and cultural appendage of the Iberian peninsula provoked an era of emulation of European language, and consequently, the imitation of genres. The result is a juxtaposition of identities and loyalties, and subsequent literary vehicles—novels, poetry, and theater—are not indigenous; they have been imported from Spain and are the product of creative forces that wish to be heard and do so by adjusting themselves to external conventions. The church and the viceregal state, hoping to make the new land a place equal or similar to the Motherland, set these forces in motion, sometimes promoting them, other times censoring them.

This cultural adaptation is, in reality, the leitmotif of Ibero-American art. The dichotomy of the foreign models and the loyalty to idols or native idiosyncracy is ever-present in the veins of the intelligentsia even now. Thus, the idea of parody is well entrenched in this culture, not always via humor but through variation, stylization, appropriation, and, above all, by way of the generic memory, to which the writers of Mexico City, Río de la Plata, Lima, or Bogotá come to feed themselves. Lizardi's *The Itching Parrot;* "El matadero" (The Slaughterhouse), the story-chronicle from the Unitarian encyclopedist Esteban Echeverría; the poems of the Venezuelan Andrés Bello, the "intellectual father" of the American republics; the modern art of Rubén Darío, Manual Gutiérrez Nájera, Julián del Casal, and José Martí—these and all the literary manifestations in the continent are permeated, in one form or another, by a longing for equality before the European progenitor.

Modernism serves as an interpretive key: from Darío's *Azul . . .* (1888) to José Enrique Rodó's *Ariel* (1900), the movement yearned for a cosmopolitan spirit and a language free from the odious celebratory parochialism of the exploits of French symbolism. Monegal asserts that Darío used a linguistic repertoire "to construct a model that not only was foreign to him . . . , but also to the everyday world of his readers."[8] The poetic experience of the Nicaraguan was modeled after Mallarmé, Verlaine, Yeats, and Valéry, and managed to bring to Europe a literature which until then, from this side of the Atlantic, had followed the patterns of realism. The renovation of the Spanish language by Darío, and furthered by Lugones and *Lunario sentimental* (1909), prompted an integration of the French model and was a motive force, according to Bakhtin's notion of the movement of narrative genres.

Many critics have attacked these and other Europeanizing attempts, among them Hernán Vidal,[9] who has labeled authors such as Darío and Borges as "unauthentic," because they cast their eyes overseas and betray their aboriginal affiliation. This complaint makes sense; after all, there are three alternatives to the loyalty dilemma: to be "Americanist," like Arguedas, Rulfo, or the aesthetic of indigenism; to be "Europeanizing," like ultraism or modernism; or finally to reflect on the crossroad of identities, a stance assumed by Rodó in *Ariel* and continued by José Carlos Mariátegui, Pedro Henríquez Ureña, and Octavio Paz in *El laberinto de la soledad* (The Labyrinth of Solitude)—except that, in the end, they all allied themselves with one side or the other and abandoned any sense of impartiality.

As for Rodó, one can say that, through Ariel and Caliban, two characters in Shakespeare's *The Tempest*, and then *his* own Caliban, Ernest Renan, he suggests to the youth of Latin America that they should seek values that do not align them with a foreign cultural model (the United States model, which is seen as materialist and imperial) and pushes them toward a continental conscience. Paz, in turn, reflects on the historical traumas of the Mexican in this book from 1950, evaluates his ambiguity and servitude under outside forces (Spain, France, the United States), and as a conclusion he proposes to assume an identity of confusion. "Who am I?" asks the Uruguayan, the Dominican, the Peruvian, and the Mexican. "A European who descended from that heartless conquistador who eradicated the native population to institute his own *modus vivendi?* Or an Aztec, Quechua, or Toltec who surrendered his land in war and peace to the white visitors from across the sea?" The range of responses is wide, and every writer's perception is determined by his own era.

Borges, the master of parody in Western culture, is a unique case: he revolutionized the language and narrative tone of the continent and maintained fidelity to Argentine themes, like the tango, the *compadrito,* the *revancha,* the *puñal,* the *gauchos,* and the *arrabales.* His parodical maneuver is extraordinary in that, by adapting and renovating, it returns to Europe and the United States a fresh, distinct, and self-aware product which makes an impression upon a broad range of novelists, academics, and storytellers, among them John Barth, Italo Calvino, Stanislaw Lem, Robert Coover, and Umberto Eco. The aforementioned Pierre Menard serves as a multicultural paradigm, not only because he rewrites the magnum opus of a Spaniard, Cervantes, the narrative germ from which emanates every Latin American novel, but because Borges makes Menard a Frenchman, and furthermore a symbolist, as if he were dealing with a postmodernist (this term understood in the Ibero-American sense) revenge. For Menard, *Don Quixote* is a work that belongs to an environment external to his; to reproduce it, he should learn Castillian, he should "pretend to inhabit" the seventeenth century.[10] He is obliged to produce one linguistic translation and another cultural. Barth himself, the North American novelist, author of *LETTERS*, discusses this character's exploration of parody in "The Literature of Exhaustion:"

> It would have been sufficient for Menard to attribute the novel to himself in order to have a new work of art, from the intellectual point of view. Indeed, in several short stories Borges plays with this very idea, and I can readily imagine Beckett's next novel, for example, as *Tom Jones*, just as Nabokov's recentest was his multivolume annotated translation of Pushkin.[11]

Menard's adaptation is less his and more a product of the times, because between the seventeenth and nineteenth centuries there is more of a difference among readers than creators, which accounts for the chasm between one *Quixote* and the other. Thus Borges parodies parody; he invents a self-parody. By doing so, he draws an intellectual map insinuating that writers sometimes adapt genres, other times just rewrite. Originality, then, is null; the same is true of authenticity. Barth goes one step farther: he suggests that such self-parodying productions occur everyday, everywhere; it is a recurrent mechanism in modern (or postmodern, in the Anglo-Saxon sense) culture. That which distinguishes a past work from a contemporary one is sometimes just the title, or a few details. In the second half of the twentieth century our cultural world, at times baroque and "counterreformist" like that of Cervantes, feels a fascination toward the art of variations, adaptations, rewritings, the art of multiple levels of reading—in sum, fascinated by the myriad of possibilities of parody.

That Borges's pseudo-essay was written in 1939 is symptomatic. Even though the literature of Latin America has always been an irremediable product of Europe, two decades after Pierre Menard parodical mechanisms aligned themselves with the Boom featuring Julio Cortázar, Carlos Fuentes, García Márquez, José Donoso, and Mario Vargas Llosa. Based on playful approximations and using various exotic settings, some authors, deliberately or not, attempted to rewrite archaic books and aged ideas and adapt long literary traditions. Through this remodeling of myths and old ghosts, these authors gave renewed spirit to the novel and the short story, both of which, according to critics, were exhausted and breathing their last gasps in Europe with Joyce, Robert Musil, Marcel Proust, and Franz Kafka. Most authors had worked as journalists or professors and their literary culture was broad and substantial. The influences of Faulkner, Poe, Hemingway, the Robbe-Grillet's *nouveau roman*, Claude Simon, and Nathalie Serrault, surrealism and the Russian and Nordic writers all infused their lectures and conversations, and manifested themselves the moment they began to write.[12]

One exemplary work among many is *La guerra del fin del mundo* (The War of the End of the World) by Peruvian Mario Vargas Llosa. It is essentially a reconsideration, an adaptation. Within its pages it depicts a mosaic of religious and economic conflicts, inspired by *Os Sertões* (Rebellion in the Backlands, 1902) by Euclides da Cunha, which is based on the rebellion of Canudos in 1896 by the *cangaceiros* forces (composed of fugitive slaves, underprivileged civilians, bandits, and so on), and the fanaticism toward their charismatic leader, Antonio Conselheiro, whose coup was quickly and dispassionately suppressed by the Brazilian national army. Da Cunha, whose personal biography is a succession of tragic accidents (like that of Horacio Quiroga), worked as a reporter for the newspaper *Estado de São Paulo*. In the Spanish edition of *The War of the End of the World* there appears an illustration of Conselheiro, and his journalistic chronicle plays a critical role in the second half, serving as counterpoint to the situation as perceived by the press of Bahía, especially by the *Jornal de Noticias*, in 1897. Mario Vargas Llosa spent a year of investigation at the Wilson Center and read everything the Library of Congress had about Canudos; as a result his information is more precise than da Cunha's. The 5,200 *jagunços* in the Brazilian's version became 5,783 in the Peruvian's; the documentation and history were transformed into fiction, an entangled, accumulative narration. The result is a kind of recycled material where our commonly understood definition of originality—the creation of an idea ex nihilo—remains hazy. And the book is disquieting because Vargas Llosa does not imitate a European model, but a Brazilian one that shares his peripheral existence.

Other cases of parodical stylization are *¿Quién mató a Palomino Molero?* (Who Killed Palomino Molero?), which toys with detective fiction; Julio Cortázar's stories "La puerta condenada" and "Historia con migalas," which revalued (employing a fantastical, not psychological, reading) gothic literature and the horror of H. P. Lovecraft and Edgar Allan Poe (the Argentine, one must remember, translated the complete works of Poe); *Tres tristes tigres* (Three Trapped Tigers), Cabrera Infante's carnivalesque novel; the influx of the foilletons from Manuel Puig, *Cristopher Unborn*, which translates, reorders, renews, and adapts a text which by itself is a carnival; and Lawrence Sterne's *Tristram Shandy*. Also among these is Fuentes's novella *Aura*, from 1962, which, as the author has announced in his "How I Wrote One of My Books" (*Myself with Others*, 1988), is a rewriting of the philosophical and poetic approximations of Quevedo, Henry James, Borges and the *nouveau roman*, on top of, clearly, drawing from personal experience.

The time has come to view parody as a creative force in Latin America and Fuentes's case is perhaps the best because he has reflected upon this parodying tendency in his work as an essayist. The following commentary discusses his attachment to Quevedo:

> You have already noticed, of course, that the true author of *Aura* . . . is named Francisco de Quevedo y Villegas, born on September 17, 1580, in Madrid and supposedly deceased on September 8, 1645, in Villanueva de los Infantes; the satirical and scatological brother of Swift, but also the unrivaled poet of our death and love, our Shakespeare, our John Donne, the furious enemy of Góngora, the political agent from the Duke of Osuna, the unfortunate, jailed partisan of fallen power, the obscene, the sublime Quevedo dead in his stoical tower, dreaming, laughing, searching, finding some of the truly immortal lines in the Spanish language:

> > Oh condición mortal Oh dura suerte
> > Que no puedo querer vivir mañana
> > Sin la pensión de procurar mi muerte.

> > (Oh immortal state Oh man's unyielding fate
> > To live tomorrow I can have no hope
> > Without the cost of buying my own death.)

Or maybe these lines, defining love:

> > Es yelo abrasador, es fuego helado,
> > es herida que duele y no se siente,
> > es un soñado bien, un mal presente,
> > es un breve descanso muy cansado.

(It is a freezing fire, a burning ice,
it is a wound that hurts yet is not felt,
a happiness desired, a present evil,
a short but, oh, so tiring rest.)

Yes, the true author of *Aura* is Quevedo, and I am pleased to represent him here today.

This is the great advantage of time: the so-called author ceases to be such; he becomes an invisible agent for him who signed the book, published it, and collected (and goes on collecting) the royalties. But the book was written—it always was, it always is—by others.[13]

The final affirmation encapsulates the superimposition of originalities, the replacement of an antique one for one more contemporary. *Aura* and its author, then, are symbols of the insatiable hunger to revise the literary past through new narrative experiments.

The critical role of the Boom, whatever its commercial and propagandistic motives may have been, was that it removed the continent's literature from the periphery and, as Bakhtin did to Dostoyevsky, put it at centerstage. Such relocation was not gratuitous, like Rodríguez Monegal explains in the preface to volume 2 of his *Borzoi Anthology of Latin American Literature*. The end of World War II brought with it the decline of European colonialism as the intellectual headquarters of operations.

Peripheral realities, absent from Eurocentric imagination for centuries, began to evidence themselves and attract attention, and they did it almost in unison with the emergance of independence movements in areas of Oceania, Africa, Asia, South America, and even Central Europe—wherever the imperial-colonial relationship was no longer effectual. It was before this backdrop that a new type of novel arose, one which distanced itself from the bourgeois realist prototype immortalized by Austen, Stendhal, and Flaubert, or from the "decadent" of Joyce, Musil, Proust, and Kafka.

Renovating voices and airs became evident in these peripheral zones, represented by Nadine Gordimer, V. S. Naipaul, Chinua Achebe, Salman Rushdie, and Milan Kundera, among others. Also of great import were Miguel Angel Asturias, the Guatemalan who received the Nobel Prize in 1967, and his contemporaries who followed him into the international arena. (Although Darío had already arrived in Europe a half-century earlier and was the only Ibero-American who had achieved such a deed outside of Spain, because of his connection with Juan Ramón Jiménez, the truth is that his work was never taken seriously.) Here is where one must place the literary Boom, which, to paraphrase the bolivarian dream, united the chroniclers of Peru with those of Colombia, the Argentines with the Mexicans. It was a phase of cultural transfer that managed to redefine the concepts of center, periphery, and intellectual control. Above all, the European novel, instead of influencing, saw itself influenced by currents that came from those lands once walked by Lope de Aguirre, Francisco Pizarro, and Bernal Díaz del Castillo.

Decades later, however, the Boom's originality should not be seen through such a clear lens: its ludic craving, its bookish tone, its tribute to European or North American trends, and its idealization of the Borgesian mockery of universal culture, all prompted writers to embrace the art of rewriting. There is nothing bad in it—when all is said and done, the talent and experimental eye of those who conformed it generated products of outstanding quality. Rodríguez Monegal said:

These new perceptions in the West have found a parallel in the discovery by the nations of the so-called Third World that high culture is not the privilege of any given race or country, that it exists in many forms, and, moreover, that one method of producing an original culture in a colonized society is by thoroughly parodying—and thus destroying, and thus re-creating—the culture of the colonizers.

To the performance of this task Latin Americans have brought, and bring, obvious advantages. For nearly four centuries their writers and thinkers have devoted themselves, with the help of Indians, blacks, and assorted Europeans, to the production of a new Iberian culture on this side of the Atlantic. They succeeded in creating their own variety of Baroque, and anticipated their peninsular counterparts in adapting to their own purposes the techniques and insights of parnassianism, symbolism and naturalism. In this century, they became involved in the work of the international avant-garde, in the development if the nouveau roman, and even in the founding of a new school of criticism. Latin Americans have, at long last, become true contemporaries, if not in fact the vanguard, of all mankind.[14]

The explorations of Pierre Menard in undertaking the incredibly complex task of repeating a pre-existing book in a foreign language remain as a metaphor for the phenomenon of the parody discussed by Bakhtin. In the hands of Fuentes, García Márquez, Vargas Llosa, Cortázar, and their following, it has been taken one step farther: they have enriched through deliberate anachronisms, the adaptation of foreign texts allowed them to renovate, and they have turned literature into a universal dialogue of books, languages, and times.

The detective novel, then, is that "subgenre" which was so attractive after Tlatelolco in Mexico (and in other parts of the continent, descendants of the Boom), which utilizes those parodical mechanisms to adapt an imported formula to its new surroundings, whether through pure "stylization," or using more original skills like "variation" or the "parodical stylization." In other words, from the mere translations of Sherlock Holmes and Hercule Poirot to the creation of native private eyes, a slow metamorphosis has come about, a distillation where detective literature, albeit derived from borrowed attitudes and behavior, has acquired its own personality.

3

ABC, or the Formula

WHAT characteristics determine a detective novel? How can a reader distinguish one? Are there variations on the same structure? To ease understanding, there are four principal components which, from here forward, I will call "the formula:"

1. SUSPENSE, which the writer achieves through the slow and calculated revelation of information. "The Murders in the Rue Morgue" is a perfect example: the detective, C. Auguste Dupin, is confronted with a series of incidents around two murders whose victims are a mother and a daughter, and everything seems to indicate that the perpetrator is a lunatic. Eventually, through clues, proofs, and guesswork, he discovers that he is dealing with an orangutan. The evidence does not come to light until the end, and the information is well hidden to keep the reader attentive. Poe offers clues that are selective, ordered, manipulative, and elusive, and the act of unveiling the truth is also that of opening it. Truth is synonymous with revelation, and revelation demands patience and manipulation. The author is in candid superiority over his creations as well as the reader; he, and nobody else, knows the result of the deduction before it comes to fruition. Dickens and William Godwin, two of Poe's precursors, never elaborated the method; their suspense was derived from social tension, realistic descriptions, and the characters' psychology (Caleb Williams, especially). "The Murders" was the text that established the basis for the idea of detection.

But this is far from our notion of common, traditional suspense, which comes from natural or supernatural fear, or unsatisfied love—properties of gothic and romance novels. Detective literature replaces these fears with unanswered questions. In *The Pursuit of Crime*, Dennis Porter attempted to analyze the structural motives of the detective story. He argues that the reader's anxiety, resulting from hidden and thus unresolved situations, depends upon the time that elapses between a sequence's initiation and

43

the approach to its conclusion, the sympathy that the characters provoke, the nature of the threat seen in the obstacles, and the desire for resolution. Suspense will be perpetuated as long as there is imminent danger. And he says:

> More obviously than most other fiction or drama, a detective novel is composed of two contradictory impulses. On the one hand, it is made up of verbal units that combine to close the logico-temporal gap between a crime and its solution. On the other hand it also contains an equal number of units that impede progress towards a solution.[1]

Spontaneity is frozen and everything is calculated, which implies that the detective genre is composed of progressions and regressions, at once centripetal and centrifugal, movements forward and backward that keep the tension in equilibrium. The writer premeditates them, plays with our logic and our conscience. A book's success depends upon the control of information and secrets, which are divulged from many different angles, through a dialectic of oppositions. Progress and the reader's curiosity, illusions and disillusions, remain balanced.

That opposition of progress and regress, as old as *Tristram Shandy,* has been utilized by the Russian formalists like Boris Tomashevsky,[2] who distinguish between "bound motifs" and "free motifs," the former being essential for the disentanglement of the plot, while the latter, which are dispensable, can (if so desired) be omitted and do not contribute to narrative progress.

2. THE USE OF A TRADITIONAL DISCURSIVE TECHNIQUE. Detective narration is similar to the coherent, linear, conservative presentation of its plot, and it rejects the unconventional. Clearly there are notable exceptions: Sophocles' *Oedipus Rex*, for example, combines the detective with the criminal; *Crime and Punishment* is narrated from the perpetrator's point of view. It would be more accurate to say that there are a number of distinguishing features which openly govern the rules and are occasionally altered. Almost without fail, however, verbal economy, restraint, and established standards are preferred. Porter believes that detective fiction's progressive and regressive elements, and the pleasure derived from them, point to legibility. The detective novel has endured as a genre primarily because, above all, it is enjoyable and "it would not be considered enjoyable by most people unless it were also easy to read."[3]

Legibility implies a continuous dialogue alternated among characters, especially the detective and his conversational partner, who verbalizes his reasoning and follows the logical steps. One also encounters colorful, colloquial language, with the exception of the hard-boiled North American writers, like Hemingway, Chandler, or Hammett, who tended to use internal monologue and coarse, prosaic, vulgar dialogue. It is in the dialogue, ultimately, where the writer establishes the bridge of identification with the reader, and where a possible nexus of class remains suggested. The rejection of experimentation and the simplicity of discourse are also visible in the selection of narrative voice: nearly always third person, omniscient, or attached to one character, so the writer may achieve an "objective" perspective of the action.

3. THE CAST OF TYPICAL AND MANNEQUIN-LIKE CHARACTERS, which includes a reluctant, antisocial, but intelligent and suspicious detective, a sidekick (or a few) who seek the services of the investigator, usually a layperson or scientist. There is also at least one thief or criminal, not to mention suspects, witnesses, and supernumeraries. From moral and psychological perspectives, the characters are archetypal caricatures of good, evil, reason, stupidity, or violence. They, in the hands of a reductionist writer, are made superficial and with minimal personality. They react to the world in predictable ways, like parts of a machine whose end justifies the means.

4. MORALITY AND INTELLECT. Reason always triumphs over irrationality and order over disorder. Similarly, from Poe to Chesterton, the human elements in detective writing will end up victorious, while the chaos of the universe is subjected to a rigorous intellectual plan. Using the deductive method of Occam's philosophy (clearly seen in *The Name of the Rose* by Umberto Eco), the detective always manages to "deduce" the truth, as in the works of Conan Doyle or Sayers. Deduction is a syllogistic mental process through which the investigator makes connections, combines premises, and arrives at conclusions.

Take, for example, *A Study in Scarlet*. In the beginning, after Holmes has only known Watson for a few minutes, he tells him, "You have been in Afghanistan, I perceive." Obviously, Watson is dumbstruck by such shrewdness, above all because nobody knew of his trip. He asks for an explanation and gets one: "From long habit the train of thoughts ran so swiftly through my mind that I arrived at the conclusion without being conscious of intermediate steps," says Holmes. "There were such steps, however." And he outlines his observations: a doctor with a military air; ergo an army doctor; a darkened or suntanned countenance; wounded and sick.

"Where in the tropics could an English army doctor have seen much hardship and got his arm wounded? Clearly in Afghanistan."[4]

This type of deduction can be correct or incorrect—the latter is based on a false premise or inappropriate syllogism—but one as much as the other results in suspense. At the core of the book there always lies a question. To answer it means to expose the truth and organize the chaos, that is, the artificial order imposed by the criminal. At the end, truth and good dominate; thus the genre can be recognized as moralist. Human reason knows the unknown, the enigmas of the universe are exposed, and the criminals go to jail. In the espionage novel this morality still prevails, but the deduction is replaced by persecution and physical combat. The opposition of good and bad is reduced to a confrontation of political, scientific, or financial forces.

The sum of all the aforementioned narrative ingredients, according to many, makes global structure overwhelm the characters, who seem mere gears within clockwork, and eliminates the emotional dimension.

Roger Caillois, in *The Poetics of Murder* (1941), discusses this intellectual element and its ambiguity toward man and his existence. He elaborates a hypothesis which is based on five questions: who, when, where, why, and how; that is to say, five coordinates: the protagonist, the drama, the spatial-temporal dimension, and the psycho-sociological motives.

> The novel and the detective novel are therefore totally different: the first takes human nature as its basis and its subject, while the second only reluctantly admits human nature because it must. The detective novel would abolish human nature altogether if it could. In fact, however, it keeps quite a lot of what it wishes it could banish, and profits from the retention. It is only because the detective novel, however much it wishes it were an intellectual puzzle, remains a novel that attracts so many readers who are indifferent to the charms of geometry. In spite of everything, it is necessary to speak of death, of murder, of violence. The detective novel must have a hero and it must recount a drama. It is a strange ambiguity that a genre with such strictly abstract ambitions ends up interesting its readers by such obvious emotional attractions.[5]

Caillois asserts that the five questions do not have the same validity because *who* and *how* predominate, which implies that man must be discussed within his own context. As in any realist novel, the writer personalizes his work through a caricaturing and superficial tone, or by injecting vivacity, depth, and candor into his creations.

4

Brief Overview

WHAT comprised the foreign model, the European or North American genre which, upon reaching Mexico, inspired local efforts?

A patient, meticulous history of the vast genealogical network of mystery and detective literature would be infeasible here, in that it is difficult to distinguish between high quality works (which cannot be reduced to a simple formula or the mere manipulation of archetypes) and lesser texts, and also because the range of themes and ethnic heritages is truly overwhelming. Instead, I will attempt a review, a synthesis (albeit reductionist) of the three branches or lineages in its history, from Poe to Chandler and Fleming: the sophisticated Englishman, the hard-boiled American, and the espionage novel. Since the history of any kind of literature lies more in the study and analysis of its great works than in the errors and commonalities of the lesser ones, the forgotten works, I will knowingly leave out a list of names without whom the presence of Auguste Dupin, Philip Marlowe, Miss Marple, or James Bond would have been absurd.

The year 1887 is critical; it saw the publication of *A Study in Scarlet* and the inauguration of Sherlock Holmes and Doctor Watson into the literary scene. In other words, it is the year the tradition diffused from the United States and became visible in England. But, even though Arthur Conan Doyle lifted the detective to previously unconsidered fame, there are clear historical tracks and literary antecedents to be found in previous works. If one desires, it is possible to interpret *A Thousand and One Nights,* the apocryphal *Book of Daniel,* "The Clue of the Headless Corpse," from *The Histories* by Herodotus (443 B.C.), Voltaire's *Zadig* (1747), *The Adventures of Caleb Williams* by the radical thinker William Godwin (1794), "Mademoiselle de Scudéry" by E. T. A. Hoffman (1821), and *Homme au masque de fer* from Alexander Dumas (1848–50), as authentic precursors, along with Dickens's incom-

plete *The Mystery of Edwin Drood,* the only novel whose conclusion (is Edwin dead? who is the mysterious Mr. Datchery?) has
remained unresolved ad aeternum.

In each of the aforementioned works there is a secret, a crime
or attempt, and a need, social or personal, to resolve an enigma.
In addition, it is reasonable to claim that the gothic literature of
Horace Walpole's *The Castle of Otranto* (1764), Matthew Gregory
Lewis's *The Monk* (1795), Mary Shelley's *Frankenstein: or, The
Modern Promoeteus* (1818), and even Bram Stoker's *Dracula*
(1897), as another cornerstone. And it is clear: the mysterious, the
supernatural, the doubtful, and the unknown—key elements that
inhabit all that is gothic—can be found among the pages of any
nineteenth-century detective or horror novel, and even in contemporary examples. In *The Roots of Detection,* Bruce Cassiday says:

> Long before Sherlock Holmes came onto the literary scene with his
> famous explanation of the art of deduction in *A Study in Scarlet,* classic
> literature had produced isolated gems of intuitive reasoning, strewing
> them amidst the fables, myths, and legends that make up humanity's
> reservoir of written knowledge.[1]

One can claim, at least in the abstract, a juxtaposition of Godwin,
Shelley, and Voltaire in Sherlock Holmes, but the truth is that this
conception is not very helpful. For to travel to ages past, or to
search for the branches of a river whose thousand courses all indicate that there is indeed an ocean, does not provide us with any
reasonable conclusion.

Without question, the true titan, the pharaoh, the pillar that provided the standard that was later followed by Conan Doyle, Chesterton, Wilkie Collins, and other admirers, was Edgar Allan Poe,
who related the adventures of detective Auguste Dupin in "The
Murders in the Rue Morgue" and "The Mystery of Marie Roget"
(1841). Suspense, stereotypical characters, albeit immature, and
the triumph of reason over natural chaos, are the creations of the
North American. Other stories from Poe, like "The Golden Bug"
(1843), can also be labeled as early incursions into the genre. Poe
was the first to mix deduction with literature to produce a short
narration. His skeptical vision, his timidity, and the pain he suffered from his alcoholism made him divide reality into light and
dark, matter and spirit, and those divisions remain clear in his
essay *Eureka* (1848). Influenced by Newton and Laplace, Poe later
offered a poetic-scientific explanation of the world, at once mysti-
cal and realistic, always basing his ideas on a non-euclidean geome-

try. This work came after his fiction, but clearly illustrates his instinct toward organization, rationalization, and illumination of reality before the individual eye.

For peculiar reasons (his contemporaries, Emerson, Thoreau, and the transcendentalists, were preoccupied with other matters), Poe's contribution made no waves—he did not have any successors among his compatriots; his efforts were better received across the ocean, in France and Great Britain.

With the 1920 prohibition of alcohol in the United States (Roosevelt repealed Hoover's 18th amendment in 1933), urban crime skyrocketed. At one level, the amount of street violence increased as unemployed workers sought food and security. Meanwhile, the criminal element organized into mafias and urban gangs, with which Al Capone and Dutch Schultz, among others, were affiliated. In England, G. K. Chesterton, Agatha Christie, and Dorothy L. Sayers explored Poe's model, and the genre followed the norm of cold calculation, never naturalism or realism. When it again crossed the ocean and settled in New York and Chicago, the rash of urban violence brought with it a growth of the organs of political control, and the old intelligent, calm detective relinquished his chair to the rude, cruel investigator for whom anything goes (sleeping with women, abusing the defenseless, acceptance of corruption, and so on) in the effort to restore order and solve a crime. Often these investigators, Charlie Chan or Ellery Queen for instance, worked for themselves, outside of the police. Their British precursors were always of the upper class, with their material needs already met; the growing educated middle class provided the audience, and the theater of their actions never involved issues of social instability.

The opposite branch, the realist and prosaic, the North American, mixed among the lower class—slums, trash, brothels, misery, and violence—and soon acquired the nickname "dirty realism." Its best examples were Hemingway's "The Killers" (1937), Dashiell Hammett's *The Maltese Falcon,* published in the magazine *Black Mask* between September 1929 and January 1930, and Raymond Chandler's *The Big Sleep* (1939). The language they used was vulgar and ambiguous, as was the morality of their characters. Brutality and corruption, especially in the upper class, were its themes. The term "detective" was soon replaced by "private eye," which referred to a starving investigator who was well versed in gunplay and familiar with the underworld. Although these private eyes fought for what was right, their dignity was suspect. This new roster of crude and aggressive investigators was headed by Chandler's

Philip Marlowe. In his article "The Simple Art of Murder" in the December 1944 issue of *Atlantic Monthly,* Chandler recognized this direction of the genre and cited Hammett as its principal promoter, but it was he himself who immortalized it, with his disposition toward coarseness and his love-hate relationship with Los Angeles, the site of his adventures.

Previously, I mentioned Al Capone and Dutch Schultz. Their names are important in that they demonstrate how Christie, Chesterton, and Conan Doyle concerned themselves with individual criminality while Hammett and Chandler dealt with organized crime, the Italian mafias, the logistical attacks upon the government. The gangster became the nemesis, and, although his public aggressions were the stuff of newspaper stories and diplomatic scandals, dirty realism's task was to convert them into literature. Julian Symons, one of the most outstanding critics of the detective tradition, says in his *Bloody Murder:*

> The American revolution made the hard-boiled crime story respectable. *Red Harvest* and *The Maltese Falcon* were recognized as new, remarkable, and American . . . With the groundwork thus laid, the crime story could be treated as literature. Raymond Chandler (1888–1959) was highly conscious of the fact that he was working in what he called a mediocre form and trying to "make something like literature out of it". Such implicit contempt for what you are doing is not a good receipt for any kind of writing, yet Chandler succeeded.[2]

The true explosion of the detective genre occurred at the end of World War II, with the arrival of Simon and Schuster's "pocketbook" in the United States, which prompted the production of books in series—the "dime novel" in North America and the "pennydreadful" in England had been the thematic and commercial precursors—and also in massive numbers. With this new approach to retail, the market grew from a quantifiable number of readers to an almost infinite one in the blink of an eye. Publishers made the genre more lucrative for the writers, and elevated them to the stature of superstars. The two parallel factions, the cold and elegant (British), and the dirty and realistic (North American) soared to new heights. Both diffusion and prestige, if nothing else, inspired the third vein: that of espionage novels, which gestated between the wars. This emergence denotes a transition from organized and state crime to international violence, above all between the western and communist worlds.

Symons traces its origins to *The Spy* (1821) by James Fenimore Cooper. The subgenre achieved an early separation at the end of the twenties under the pen of Somerset Maugham, although the coterie of its outstanding authors came only with the Cold War, led by John LeCarré and *The Spy Who Came in From the Cold* (1963), and various novels by Graham Greene, Morris West, Frederick Forsyth, and Robert Ludlum.

The spy is the detective who defends the sovereignty of the civilized world against the forces of evil, represented by the Soviet Union, Islam, or science in a maniac's hands. The mystery is not based on the identity of the criminal, but his degree of infamy; the questions to answer, then, are not who nor why, but when and where. James Bond, an agent for the British Secret Service, who was born in *Casino Royale* (1953), and whose ethical and semiotic mechanisms were studied by Umberto Eco, is perhaps the most famous spy.[3] Unlike his counterparts in Agatha Christie or Chandler, he is a superman: more intrepid than intelligent, he knows how to overcome any obstacle, which elevates him to an almost immortal level; he is physically agile and knows martial arts; he has the technology to destroy his opposition; he feels superior to women, minorities, and even his own chief; and the places he frequents are multifaceted and multilingual, although he tends to homogenize them. Furthermore, his language is always sparing: he is more action than talk.

These are the three veins. It is important to note that the popularization of the genre, starting in the thirties, is also a result of cinema. Furthermore, it must be added that detective literature represents a mix of popular culture and minority culture (select, but not sophisticated), because, although this type of literature reaches many readers, it always finds a select public.

Mexican literature, as the reader will discover in the next chapter, despite drawing from all three veins, favors the second and third, dirty realism and espionage novels. A crude, slow, and eclectic detective, who works for himself, outside of the government, who fights the criminals and the police at the same time, and who deals with the infiltration of spies or foreign interests, adapts more easily to the national atmosphere.

In Buenos Aires, due to the Europeanizing spirit of the culture, the opposite occurred. Ever since *Con la guadaña al hombro* by Diego Ketliber, the pseudonym of Abel Mateo (1940), one of the genre's first attempts in South America, inspired by Ellery Queen, and where the nickname "fair play"—to avoid deliberately misleading the reader—arose, the intellectual side always has been celebrated. Among the standouts in the Argentine literary showcase are the art of Borges and Bioy Casares, *El estruendo de las*

rosas by Manuel Peyrou (1948), *Las nueve muertes del Padre Metri*
by Padre Leonardo Castellani (1942), the pseudonym of Jerónimo
del Rey, who admired Father Brown, and *Seis problemas para don
Isidro Parodi* (Six Problems for Don Isidro Parodi) from the same
year, in which, despite the comic, colorful, and indigenous language that abounds, he is so dominated by intellectualism that he
must impose handicap: his detective is imprisoned and solves
crimes from his cell.

In Mexico, although emulations of Chesterton and Conan Doyle
do exist, idiomatic experiments have stood out, satire *à la* Cantin-
flas and novels *à la* Chandler and LeCarré.

Part 2

5

Constables and Sentries

In *Delightful Murder: A Social History of the Crime Story* (1984), Ernest Mandel states that the appearance and popularization of the detective genre in France and England can be attributed to the emergence, within urban-bourgeois societies, of a corps of detectives in police forces specializing in the investigation and control of public crime. This suggests that political circumstances demanded the genesis of a civil officer. The Belgian socialist critic studies the increased violence in London and Paris at the beginning of the nineteenth century, and his analysis focuses on Paris of 1835, when 237 individuals were convicted of criminal acts; there were another 375 in 1847, and 444 in 1868. Mandel examines the impact of this soaring criminality in the works of Dickens and Balzac, and says that it occurred before, during, and after the worker's revolt in the silk factory of La Croix-Rousse in Lyon, from 1830 to 1848. The disturbance led officials to extreme solutions, transforming the police force into a spy ring to monitor the assemblies and demonstrations of the labor leaders. "The nature of the original detective story," asserts Mandel, "is thus related equally to the functions of popular literature and to the deeper forces operating beneath the surface of bourgeois society. The reduction of crime, if not of human problems themselves, to 'mysteries' that can be solved is symbolic of a behavioural and ideological trend typical of capitalism."[1]

This socioeconomic perspective is engaging. Death and the safety of the individual in bourgeois society are two elements that mold the frontiers of the genre, and political desire to control the eruptions of insanity, crime, and psychological and collective instability is intimately connected to the concerns surrounding detective modes. This serves an assuaging purpose, providing testimony and/or evidence that bourgeois morality, as much as the structures of capitalist production and the role of the State, was adequate in the past and made a significant impact on literature.

We can read police texts like *The Mystery of Edwin Drood* or *The Moonstone* as artifacts of the increase in police control over the masses and the governmental role in the organization and establishment of the moral and civic order; they demonstrate civilization's struggle to contain madness, chaos, and anarchy. It is important to factor in the legal/medical elements derived from positivism, which assert that there is a criminal "type," that delinquency is inborn, as the naturalistic characters created by Balzac and Zola demonstrate. According to Walter Benjamin, in 1840 the invention and popularity of photography and the use of ink-based fingerprints contributed to the consolidation of this policial phalanx.[2] The German attributes the public attention he received largely to this apparent moral decay and to widespread curiosity about whether or not the police force and its techniques were effective.

In non-European countries, these ideas are only half right. Any literary work, from the Bible to *Macbeth* or *One Hundred Years of Solitude,* is based on certain moral patterns and human symbols—love, death, revenge, hate, spiritual pilgrimage, and so on. The roots of the detective genre, I have already explained, penetrate deep into the philosophies of William of Occam and in Catholic and Lutheran ideologies, which promote the dominance of the rational conscience over "the forces of the Devil."

These ingredients are transformed in fiction, metamorphized, which is not to say that they lose their abstract nature. If indeed this literature is ultimately a battle of civilized life against hysteria and disorder, only its Anglo-Saxon and French manifestations can be viewed as eyewitness testimonies to state control over society. In those countries into which the genre has arrived mediated by a bombardment of translations, television adaptations, or cinematography, there is not always a similarity between the social structures and the narratives—between reality and its artistic reflection. Capitalism in Latin America and relinquishment of the modalities of feudal society have not perished without great difficulty. Continuing political unrest has detracted from police credibility. Confidence in a state police investigator is null or minimal. Law is not a constitutional attribute without an edict from a leader who establishes the norms. Today one subscribes to a reform; tomorrow one refutes it. Justice changes hands, it is arbitrary and inconsistent, and the populace distrusts and fears official members of the political system: they view them not as civil agents, but as cogs in the wheel of the party in power—as repressors of rebellion.

Merely a glance at the Argentine chronicles and narratives from the second half of the nineteenth century or the beginning of the twentieth provides us with a sense of the fragility of the social order. Esteban Echeverría's "The Slaughterhouse," Sarmiento's *Vida de Don Facundo Quiroga* (Facundo: Civilization and Barbarism) or José Hernández's *El gaucho Martín Fierro* all demonstrate the dichotomy between the law of the State and the law of the indigents, the tension between rustic and urban life, between civilization and barbarism. After doing so, a map can be sketched depicting injustice and irrepressible partisanship struggles. Consider for a moment "The Slaughterhouse." Its publication in the *Revista del Río de la Plata* dates to 1871, almost a century after Europe had lived through the French Revolution and its consequential popular movements. Under the tyranny of restorer Juan Manuel Ortíz de Rosas, the city enters into a meat shortage of biblical proportions during Lent. The disgruntled spirits of the city-dwellers begin to boil, and those in power submit to the unitaries, "persuaded" by unspeakable tortures. As opposed to the London of Conan Doyle or the Paris of Balzac, in the Buenos Aires of "The Slaughterhouse," criminality is not an individual problem, but an ideological one. The *matasiete,* the judge and the butchers, supporters of the tyranny, are ravenous for blood. The murder that occurs is "collective" and Echeverría's description of it is valuable because it demonstrates the period of civil anarchy during independence. How, then, can one explain a genre like the detective novel, with all of its glorification of rationality and urban order, when it exists in an environment that has not yet resolved the chaos of humanity?

A perusal of the literary history of Mexico, from the Conquest to the Independence, permits one to discover that order always depends on who posseses the power. Cortés, in his *Five Letters,* and also the chronical of Bernal Díaz de Castillo, demonstrate how the Spaniard personifies law, maintaining security only in accordance with his own interests, much to the disadvantage of indigenous populations. Once and for all, the link between colonizer and colonized is disparate at economic, political, ethnic and social levels. And the same disequilibrium becomes apparent in *El fistol del diablo* by Manuel Payno, published in installments between 1845 and 1846, in which he effects an accurate criticism of the generals' lackeys who used firearms to further their own purposes, disregarding their compatriots in the process. Similar incidents transpire in the novels of the Reform (1855–1884) by Ignacio Manuel Altamirano and even in the so-called "novel of the Revolution," a movement that lasted some thirty years and included works like

Los de abajo (The Underdogs) by Mariano Azuela (1915) and *La sombra del caudillo* (1929) by Martín Luis Guzmán. The perpetuation of civilization can be traced to political friction between agrarian leaders and laborers; urban order is established by rogues and bandits, or by state servants who often promote their own interests above the common good.

The rise and fall of Demetrio Macías in *The Underdogs* is symptomatic. The arson committed by the government upon his conversion to the rebel frontlines, his liaison with intellectual Luis Cervantes, his incorporation of the ideals of the navy struggle, the capture of Zacatecas by village forces, his rank as general, and his ultimate death in Juchipila where his meteoric career began—all of the above represent the failure of social stability, the *arriviste* element of the military and the farcical nature of morality. Similarly, in the book by Martín Luis Guzmán featuring the fictitious General Ignacio Aguirre, minister of war during Caudillo's presidency (based on the regime of Plutarco Elías Calles, 1924–28), the protagonist once again is the embodiment of selfish ambition. If indeed Azuela concentrates on the life of the humble citizen, whom one observes grovelling to a *mare magnum* of guerillas, Guzmán focuses his efforts on a reenactment of the political intrigues and demonstrates how the slightest disloyalty to the leader inevitably ends in the traitor's capture and execution.

It must be emphasized, then, that in a chronic climate of agitation and fragile civil equilibrium, the rise of the private detective complicates because the border between good and evil lacks rigidity and oscillates with the atmosphere of the moment.

Perhaps due to the relative stability of Buenos Aires and the textured underworld of that great metropolis, the first manifestations of this type of literature—the crime novel genre—in Latin America appear in "El candado de oro" (The Golden Padlock, 1884) by Paul Groussac, and "El triple robo de Bellamore" (The Triple Robbery of Bellamore, included in *El crimen del otro,* 1903), a collection by Horacio Quiroga, a writer of obvious literary influence.

Argentina would produce its first novel, *El enigma de la calle Arcos* by Sauli Lostal, in 1932. More than a decade before, *El misterio* (1920) appeared, collaboratively written by Afranio Peixoto, Viriato Correa, José Joaquím de Campose Medeiros e Alburquerque, and Henrique Maximiniano Coehlho Neto. (There is another modern novel, with a chapter by João Guimarães Rosa, the title of which is *O misterio de M.)* But the genre would crystallize until the forties. Thus, between "The Murders in the Rue Morgue" and "Death and the Compass" by Borges, although there is recurrent interaction between the North American and Argentine text, there is also an embryogenesis, a process of incubation.

Capitalism transformed the mechanisms of control in the developed world, and this transformation expressed itself in the novels of Sherlock Holmes and Fantômas. In the nations in which socioeconomic development has been slow and halting, the genre appeared thanks to a literary dialogue with foreign novels, because, while capitalism consolidated its methods of social control in Latin American countries, its writers—modernists, symbolists, or parnassians—were preoccupied by other aesthetic topics. And because in those countries cultural penetration has created a hybrid population that enables the identification of certain stereotypes, writers like Paco Ignacio Taibo II, to satisfy some internal obsession or perhaps in the name of narrative experimentation, invented their detectives in order to set in motion the deductive machine, positioning them within the national idiosyncracy.

They demonstrate, then, a kind of "anti-Semitism without Jews": despite the fact that Buenos Aires, Mexico or Colombia's investigators either didn't exist or weren't trustworthy, they were invoked nevertheless. In Spain, for example, where during the reign of Franco the police were perceived as oppressors, Manuel Vásquez Montalbán's Carvahlo or the anonymous detective of Eduardo Mendoza arrived at the scenes of crimes, not in imitation of real-life role models, but rather based on earlier characters, among them those of Hammett and Chandler. Erik Lönnrot, Borges's detective, and Isidro Parodi, the detective jointly created by Bioy Casares and Borges, were not inspired by the everyday reality of Río de la Plata, but rather by Poe and Father Brown of Chesterton. The same phenomenon occurred in Mexico, where, as we will explore shortly, after the presidency of Lázaro Cárdenas (1936–40) the police forces lost public respect and slid into corruption. The appearance of detectives like Péter Pérez or Héctor Belascoarán Shayne could not have been (nor were they) inspired by Mexico's own police force. Rather, they were modeled after foreigners.

This development carries with it an implicit attack upon the governing regimes (of Perón, Franco, and so on), repressive controlling techniques and policial corruption. One can deduce that in these latitudes, the genre contains a heavy dosage of subversive thought and antistate criticism—and that, in fact, it flourishes in "hard-boiled" literature, one of the three strains of detective fiction.

In whatever form, it is worthwhile to ask when the first real policemen and detectives appeared in Mexico. From Tenochtitlán, with its jurisprudence center in Coyohuacan in the Plaza Mayor, the early center of Mexico City, the existence of police figures in the modern sense of the term was not recorded until the beginning of this century. During the pre-Columbian period in the Aztec empire, public authority figures existed called *alguaciles* who performed the functions of a police force. These officials were appointed at the behest of the *calpullis,* who regulated security and kept the peace among fellow citizens and between zones bordering the metropolis. Their role was limited to curbing depravity and reducing crime. These *aguaciles* were required to report their activities to judiciaries in their respective villages.

After 1525, the troops of Hernán Cortés replaced them with custodians, who both swept the floors of the new prisons and brought villains before the town council. The arrival of the Spaniards also brought the penetration of Renaissance ideas about the state and sovereignty, ideas that were primarily based upon *The Prince* by Machiavelli. The soldiers, subordinates loyal to the emperor, were charged with the maintenance of order. In New Spain, these gubernatorial representatives were given free reign to punish and reward without the imposition of a restraining constitution or regulations. The Crown needed them to defend the territory. But according to Mark A. Burkholder and Lyman L. Johnson, who analyzed the transition from militia to police force in *Colonial Latin America,*[3] in 1540 there appeared a decree that ordered "all able-bodied men" to serve in the military if called upon to do so. As they were waiting, the Spaniards and Creoles determined who would enlist, and eventually the mixed-bloods and Indians in the territory were drafted by the colonial authorities. They were to act as soldiers, yet they lacked the rank of a subject directly from Spain. When the number of new soldiers multiplied, the Crown had problems furnishing rations and munitions. Because the royal laws prohibited importing arms, they had to come directly from the Crown's orders, and the viceroys continually grumbled about the shortage of supplies.

In addition to the *alguaciles,* the *serenos* or night were watchmen responsible for shouting a crime and/or robbery out loud, though they were not involved with control or interference. According to Burkholder and Johnson, what the government spent in defense was minimal during the sixteenth century and a good portion of the seventeenth; the quantity, however, soon increased at a high rate. "By 1640 the Mexican treasuries were spending a third or more of their revenues on defense, as they provided heavy subsidies to the Caribbean and Phillipines as well as for the defense of Mexico itself. By the late seventeenth century, military expenditures regularly exceeded the treasuries' remission of bullion to Spain."[4] This situation prevailed until 1789, when the Count of Revillagigedo, then-viceroy of New Spain, ordered the creation of a detachment responsible for guarding Mexico City. He assured that the members would be trained, disciplined, and uniformed.

According to Arturo Sotomayor, in an article discussing the birth of the police force in Mexico in the magazine *Comunidad Conacyt*,[5] a legal entity began to emerge at the end of the seventeenth century in the form of a sort of rural police dubbed *La Acordada* composed primarily of natives and some mixed-bloods. It was established by a viceroyal accord between 1711 and 1716 by the Duke of Linares, both to control the population and to establish order. This official body eventually replaced the conquistadors as disciplinarian forces, much like the soldiers that the authorities within the Colony had requested. And Burkholder and Johnson said that by the time the English captured Havana in 1762, there were very few soldiers in service in the colonies, including New Spain. The forces that defended the coasts north of the Gulf of Mexico against buccaneers and pirate ships (like those of John Oxenham or Francis Drake) were composed of security guards who patrolled the fortresses and presidios. The total militia there during this period, counting those from New Spain, Río de la Plata and southern Chile, barely came to a few thousand men.[6]

Sotomayor states that in independent Mexico in circa 1821, due to budget exigencies, citizens were encouraged to safeguard social conduct on their own, thus creating the first "body of volunteer patrolmen" for the capital. The members agreed to work twenty-four-hour shifts and wear only a cutlass in a swordbelt for self-defense. These guards were active until approximately 1848, when on 20 July a decree from the minister of the interior and exterior founded the Mexico City Police Force.

When Porfirio Díaz, an admirer of anything French, took possession (1880–85) of the force, by his decree it was reorganized into the Gendarmerie of Distrito Federal Police. According to Edgardo Montiel Govea in his essay on the dark gray police uniform, they were identical to those prevalent in Paris of that time. In this period the municipal policemen called themselves the gendarmerie—from the French *gens d'arms*[7]; the populace nicknamed their protectors *tecolotes* and *búhos*, eagle owls, due to the color of their uniforms and the sound of the whistles at night. Moreover, for the first time they were provided with a pistol and a long baton or club. Night cops had a lamp.[8]

During the Revolution of 1910, the Gendarmerie of Police was abolished. According to Montiel Govea, it was during this period that there were fewer than two hundred policemen in the capital, administering to the wounded with the help of the Red Cross and formally supervising national life. A large part of the peace-keeping was taken over by factions within the army, but their work was counteracted by the insurgents. Speaking of a uniformed police force, then, locates oneself in postrevolutionary Mexico.

In the government of Alvaro Obregón, Roumagnac and Benjamín Martínez, among other originators of civic security in the modern sense of the term, obtained a contract for the founding of the Technical Police Academy in 1923, which would educate young men from good families in the policial arts. The school was established on Bucareli St., no. 160. It offered courses in topography, fencing, weaponry, and basketball.[9] The school was divided into two parts: physical education and public order. Montiel Govea maintains that in 1929, when the school closed, both entities united, and it was then that various regulations and organization shifts changed its statutes.

It was during the regime of Pascual Ortíz Rubio that the Scientific Academy of Police opened on 10 July 1930, which is the authentic precursor to the actual institution that trains the *polizontes*, as these civil servants are still called. That was also the year the short-lived Female Police Force came into being, responsible for the resolution and mitigation of juvenile delinquency. From 1941 to 1942, the Academy has on record a total of 120 members, and in 1963 there were 475. Around 1972 its name was changed to Dirección de Educación Policiaca, which in 1979 moved into an institution on the Desierto de los Leones road.

From the thirties on, the police forces became permanent government bodies responsible for ensuring the safety of citizens. They were never free from accusations of association with certain splinter mafia organizations. Attacks that denounced their lax moral composition abounded during this period, and continue today—one can see proof of it in editorials and newspapers. Corruption, insufficient manpower or poor preparation, scanty interest in maintaining civil security—all problems which began during the regime of Cárdenas—have converted Mexican police into a continual target of ridicule, an organization which, at one time, engendered thoughts of artistic manifestation, collective dialogue, and projects of moral renewal within the state.

La mordida, a bribe offered to public officials, be they diplomatic, bureaucratic, or policial, is an indispensable part of the national character. Ducking past the rod of justice and into the path of corruption is a familiar route to citizens of all social levels, without class distinctions. But attacks on the authorities, along with flagging confidence, are also national traditions embedded in the collective soul. Various critics, essays, and poets have examined this idiosyncratic character trait, from Samuel Ramos's *Perfil del hombre y la cultura en México* (Profile of Man and Culture in Mexico, 1934) to the psychoanalytic studies of Santiago Ramírez (1959) and Paz's *The Labyrinth of Solitude*. Paz observes that "suspicion, dissimulation, irony, the courtesy that shuts us away from the stranger, all of the psychic oscillations with which, in eluding a strange glance, we elude ourselves, are traits of a subjected people who tremble and disguise themselves in the presence of the master."[10] The Mexican tends to perceive policemen with a mixture of repudiation, because they operate on a level above his own; fear of the force they represent, which is superior to his own; and disrespect, because he understands that the gendarme is his equal—that they sprang from the same soil. Because, via a series of historical accidents, the implementers of order (those who disrupted pre-Columbian order) always came from the outside— Spaniards, Frenchmen, North Americans, and so on—the Mexican resists believing that the organization, and its so-called security, has advantages. Given that those who rise to power usually abuse it, this failure of confidence intensifies. It follows that the Mexican continually discounts authority, that he doubts its integrity. Mexico, then, is a country in which the police exercise at best an ambiguous power.

In *Delightful Murder,* Mandel demonstrates that in Europe, especially in France and England, the detective hero originally appeared in police novels based on the archetypal figure of Vidocq, an ex-convict bandit affiliated with Napoleon's Ministry of the Interior, who, in 1828, published his *Mendaces Memorias* and apparently possessed a vengeful personality. His legend captured the popular imagination and Victor Hugo, among others, was inspired by him to create Inspector Javert in *Les Misérables*. Real life and fiction, then, are intertwined. In Mexico, however, the creation is clearly imitative, based on a foreign model adapted to national situations.

This is not to deny, however, that there are authentic investigators in the country who fulfill prosecutive tasks, and that crime-fighting history, although it is certainly of questionable morality, has generated substantial cases worthy enough to inspire the literary imagination.

6

Real-Life Cases

A<small>T</small> the end of the thirties, magazines and periodicals began to emerge, reporting detective cases in Mexico. Through other crime logs and reports, this frequently morbid, scandalous sort of exposé of events and adventures in Mexico City had already spread to degree that delighted the population.

There was the *Magazine de policía*, a tabloid periodical that was printed on Mondays and cost thirty cents. Its goal, according to the words of its subtitle, was "to reveal the defects of society in order to better it" and was "completely unattached to the bodies of public security." It commented on crimes, detentions, "horrible" cases in the country and abroad, and illustrated them with caricatures and sensationalist photographs. *Detectives: Semanario policiaco y de hechos diversos* (1932–42) claimed a similar purpose, along with *Policía internacional* (1948–63) and *Policía* (1948–54). *Alarma*, the most popular daily of this tabloid genre, began in 1951 and, dedicated to the distribution of information, detailed perverted offenses with photographs and brief texts. Thus by the time the first attempted narratives began to appear in Mexico in the forties, the reader could already rely on the surrounding media, processed or deformed by the press, for references relevant to his or her life.

Moreover, one must factor in the influences of cinematography and television. I have stated, in chapter 1, that with the end of World War II detective fiction spread to North America and England, in editions both popular and inexpensive. Two decades earlier, at the beginning of the twenties, cinema was responsible for distributing a considerable number of such adventures; since the fifties, the small screen has contributed to the task.

The first adaptation of an Agatha Christie text, *The Death of Mr. Quinn* (1928), starring Stewart Rome and Trilby Clark and directed by Leslie Hiscott, was followed by films about Hercule Poirot. *The Thin Man* by Hammett, featuring William Powell and

Myrna Loy, was directed by W. S. Van Dyke in 1934. Four years before, *Red Harvest* by Hammett (1930), almost unrecognizably, was the basis of a melodramatic comedy called *Roadhouse Nights* with Jimmy Durante and Helen Morgan under the direction of Hobart Henley.

Alfred Hitchcock, synonymous with the meeting of the police novel and the silver screen, shot to fame in 1929 with his second film *Betrayal,* starring John Longdon and Cyril Richards. Innumerable others followed, among them *Murder* (1930), *The Man Who Knew Too Much* (1934), *The Thirty-Nine Steps* (1935), and *The Lady Vanishes* (1938) with Michael Redgrave.[1] These films arrived in Mexico with subtitles no later than two years after they were made. By the fifties, the British director initiated his television series, *Alfred Hitchcock Presents,* which lasted eight seasons.

Moreover, in Mexico the adaptations to the screen were accompanied by various pocket collections, which, in the forties and fifties, were wretched translations from Buenos Aires. An example was the "Biblioteca de Oro," a tabloid-format series (like comic strips) with covers illustrated by Boc-Quet and Freixas and which sold for thirty cents at newspaper stands and bookstores. Their pages presented tales by G. K. Chesterton, S. S. Van Dine, Earl Derr Biggers, Rex Stout, Agatha Christie, E. Phillips Oppenheim, and Stuart Palmer.

The list of collections also included "Cobalto," "Débora," "Pandora," and "Linterna," four series sponsored by Malinca publishers; the "Serie Naranja" by Hachette; "Séptimo Círculo," which Borges and Adolfo Bioy Casares founded in 1945 with the Emecé publishing house; and "Rastros" and "Teseo" by Acme. The Mexican rival collections soon began to appear: "Jaguar" and "Caimán" from Editorial Diana; and "Policiaca y de Misterio," from Editorial Novaro, where Antonio Helú, the father of the detective genre there, published *La obligación de asesinar.*

Moreover, at the beginning of 1940 (20 April to be exact), Atlántida Editions launched a new product: *Novela policiaca. El mundo de crimen,* a weekly journal. It cost twenty-five cents and was published on 28 Isabel la Católica Street. It specialized in illustrated adaptations of Georges Simenon ("The Mysterious Murder of Mr. Couchet" was the first one), Gaston Boca, Raymond Fouchet, Tito Spagnol, and others. The journal was under the editorship of José Bolsa and every copy included criminal anecdotes from real life.

The leap of the printed word onto the silver screen is without a doubt one of the key factors in the genre's proliferation and popularity. In the sixties and seventies, *TV* exerted more influence than ever with series from the United States, dubbed in Spanish, like *Hawaii 5–0, Columbo, Kojak, Mannix, Petrocelli, Starsky and Hutch, Cannon, Barnaby Jones,* and *The Saint,* distributed by XEW-Channel 2.

Comics have also spread detective adventures exceedingly well. In the seventies, Novaro publishers printed *Cuentos de misterio,* with titles like "La muerte también juega," whose storylines were borrowed from Coram Nobis, Carl Wessler, and Jack Deck.

I will now focus on private eyes in the real life of the Mexican. One of the first and most celebrated Mexican detectives was Valente Quintana. A brief, though substantial, biography of his, based on the testimony of his son, has been published by its narrator and *Proceso* journalist, Carlos Borbolla.[2] Quintana had been born in 1889 in Matamoros, Tamaulipas and was the chief of police in 1929 during the regime of Emilio Portes Gil. He came from a humble family and ever since childhood had dreamed of crossing the border and finding work. He obtained a menial job in a store. In an incident not free of discrimination and racism, a client robbed some merchandise from the establishment, and the blame fell to Quintana, who was obliged to prove his innocence by exposing the guilty party. According to Borbolla, the incident, which occurred when he was seventeen years old, was a trial by fire and became his point of entry into the profession. Upon his return to the capital, he worked temporarily as a traffic policeman.

He had two nicknames: "El Zorro," and "El Sherlock Holmes Mexicano," the latter once again demonstrating dependence on foreign models. His method of capturing criminals involved disguises, and he would assume diverse masked personalities, as the occasion demanded. Under his jurisdiction were a variety of cases involving counterfeiting money and train robberies, always solved with his colleague, Alfonso Frías, at his side. His cases were reported in the media and acknowledged by the government. Perhaps the most celebrated is the assassination attempt of Portes Gil during the The Christian War in February 1929.

The president was traveling by train when dynamite blasted the railway. The explosion merely damaged the locomotive due to an error in calculation; the passengers and all of the crew disembarked unharmed, except for the engineer and his assistant. The president had been surrounded by his ministers and his closest, high-ranking diplomats, as well as a military escort. An attack had been attempted on the highest leader in the nation, and the story was covered by daily papers in both Mexico and abroad. Two sergeants were immediately dispatched to pursue the perpetrators, but they experienced little success. In a short time, Quintana and Frías were solicited, and the two detectives undertook to solve the case. They began their investigations in the vicinity of the explosion, and it didn't take long to locate a clue: A few kilometers away, they found a mud-covered membership card to an auto shop, El Puerto de Liverpool, scribbled with an address from Celaya. Their deductions took them to a potter and a devoted Christian youth. Quintana concluded by divulging the identity of the attackers; he had deduced that the attempt at destabilization and revolution was the work of masons with ties to the clergy and the Christian movement. The incident is described in three volumes detailing the history of *La Cristiada*, a.k.a. The Christian War, by Jean Meyer.[3]

The cases and adventures of Quintana became the stuff of popular folklore. His honest character, his dedication, and his incorruptibility captivated his devotees. It is probable that his techniques and schemes may have been emulations of Arthur Conan Doyle's hero. It is more doubtful, however, that his feats would have achieved such recognition at a national level had they been influenced by Borbolla.

One of the most highly debated detective cases in Mexico is the death of Trotsky (Lev Davidovich Bronstein) on 20 August 1940, in Coyoacán, a suburb south of the Distrito Federal. His body was veiled and the curious waited in long lines to pay homage to it. A sense of guilt and remorse pervaded to all levels of society and government; after all, the country had opened its doors to the expatriate in his flight from Stalin, promising a safe haven for his intellectual pursuits.

Upon the death of Lenin in the Soviet Union, Trotsky had been the legitimate successor, but Joseph Stalin had overstepped his bounds, usurping the regime and devoting himself to "purging" those members who belonged to the IV International like Zinoviev, Kamenov, Nujarin, and Rycov. Fleeing from danger and physical attacks, Trotsky sought respite in 1929 in Constantinople. Seven years later, in 1936, the Political Bureau of the International Communist League's Mexican branch sponsored Trotsky's arrival to the country, speaking through Diego Rivera and Octavio Fernández, and through the general Francisco J. Mújica, the secretary of communications and public works during the reign of Lázaro Cárdenas.

But as in a fiction of espionage and intrigue, his archenemies were already plotting a counterattack. The secret police of Stalin (the GPU) had two fervent supporters in the country: the general secretary of the Mexican labor union (the Committee of Mexican Workers, or the Consejo de Trabajadores Mexicanos), Vicente Lombardo Toledano, and David Alfaro Siqueiros, both members of the Communist Party of Mexico. Immediately, the latter attempted to persuade Cárdenas to deny entrance to Trotsky, but his efforts were in vain. He finally defected in January 1938. A mob of admirers and friends waited for Trotsky at the port of Tampico, Tamaulipas, including Diego Rivera and Frida Kahlo, who in the past had been collaborators and friends of Siqueiros. The Russian leader arrived with his spouse at his side, Natalia Sedoff, overjoyed to have escaped certain death. Some years later their grandchild, Esteban, would follow—he was the son of a son who had been assassinated while in France.

Trotsky expressed his thanks and immediately afterward settled in a house in Coyoacán, Viena No. 19. It was well-fortified with high walls and guards posted twenty-four hours a day. Even so, three years and a bit more later, on 23 May 1940, attackers penetrated within and fired at the family. All members of the family escaped unharmed, though the grandson suffered a light wound; however, Trotsky's personal secretary, Sheldon Harte, disappeared. Investigations began and Colonel Leandro A. Sánchez Salazar was assigned the case.

Later, Sánchez Salazar would be accused of ineptitude and even of conspiring with the attackers. His cunning, however, allowed the truth to be known, and the public celebrated his deeds. Sánchez Salazar discovered that Siqueiros had organized the attack. He pursued and arrested him in the state of Jalisco, then imprisoned him in Mexico City in the Lecumberri penitentiary. Carlos Monsiváis, a Mexican practitioner of New Journalism, says in one of his essays collected in *Amor perdido* (1977):

> Siqueiros' Stalinism. No one can forget the moment of the myth's ultimate ignominy, the gangster activity in which he would participate and that would define the rest of his life: On the 24th of May in 1940, Siqueiros (disguised as the head of the army) leads the commandos that immobilize the police in charge of Leon Trotsky's house in Coyoacán, the terrorists kidnap (and subsequently slay) his secretary Sheldon Harte and throw a firebomb against the apartment in which Trotsky slept. "Those"—Siqueiros later accepts an interview for the magazine *¡Ahora!*—"were very dark days, and they were full of suffering. We had just returned from the Spanish War, we were very discouraged. In the Soviet Union the struggle between Stalin and Trotsky had undermined the unity of the international Communist Movement. Our ideals were injured. We believed in the necessity of reconstructing the

ideological unity surrounding the leaders of the Kremlin." In 1940 he declares before the judge that the attempt had not been intended to inflict harm upon anyone, rather as a demonstration "directed towards exercising psychological pressure on Trotsky and inducing him to suspend his political activities."[4]

Accompanied by the Communist painter, the detective arrived at the conclusion that there was a large population of Spanish exiles in Mexico, all persecuted under Franco, among them Antonio Pujol. Eduardo Téllez Vargas, one of the reporters from the newspaper *Novedades,* traced the incidents step by step, and four decades afterwards recounted the facts in an essay called "Trotsky's Assassination," which glorifies the deeds of Sánchez Salazar.[5]

In the end, Trotsky was assassinated several months later, when an admirer of his (whose name alternates between Jacques Mornard and Frank Jackson), after giving him a manuscript for him to correct, drove an ice axe into his skull with such a force that the resulting wound was 7.5 centimeters deep. Moreover, Jackson-Mornard carried a 45-caliber pistol and a sword, and apparently was prepared to use them if necessary. Silvia Agelov, Trotsky's student and his close collaborator, was the mistress of the assassin; unbeknownst to her, she had facilitated his arrival at Viena number 19.

If indeed the "how" and "when" of the crime were rapidly established by Sánchez Salazar, the "why" remained ambiguous. Establishing it remained in the domain of a criminal specialist, Dr. Alfonso Quiroz Cuarón, another popular hero of authentic police cases. It was Quiroz Cuarón who, immediately after intense psychological and emotional assays, revealed that the real name of Mornard was Ramón Mercader del Río, that he was a native of Cataluña, as well as other particulars which are confirmed in the biography of Isaac Deutscher.[6] The efforts of Sánchez Salazar and Quiroz Cuarón culminated in putting the criminal in prison, where he served nineteen years and six months. On returning to freedom, Jackson-Mornard traveled to Havana, and from there to Czechoslovakia en route to the Soviet Union, where he was decorated for his "heroic" deeds.[7]

The cases of Valente Quintana and the scandal surrounding the assassination of Trotsky, though they are of a negative tenor, nevertheless prove that, in the Mexican context, the writing of novels about political rivals, intellectual deductions, thieves, and detectives already had a point of reference.

7

The Critic's Voice

ACCORDING to Luis Leal, the origins of the genre in Mexico go back to the forgotten novelist Alfonso Quiroga, author of *Vida y milagros de Pancho Reyes, detective mexicano.*[1] The police novel flourished in the forties in Mexico, as it did elsewhere; Rodolfo Usigli published *Ensayo de un crimen* in 1944, which many consider to be the first detective text in Mexico. Almost simultaneously to its publication, the critics began to speak up.

Argentine writer Ernesto Sábato, in his book *Heterodoxia* (1953), attacks the detective genre, stating that "in general, nobody takes it seriously; not the literati who created it—for that reason they assume pseudonyms—not the editor who produces it, nor the reader who consumes it. It is with good reason that this literature is read only by weary businessmen on airplanes."[2] Alfonso Reyes had taken the opposing standpoint a few years before:

> Until not long ago, reading detective novels was the most embarrassing form of escapism. A thing done behind closed doors, with reserve. One confessed love for these books with a smile, like he who confesses that he enjoys crossword puzzles. Some crossed swords over the detective novel. I exaggerated in 1945 to the point of saying that it was the classic genre of our time, a partial and unpopular truth, as Chesterton would define it. I exaggerated out of anger at the hypocrisy and as a healthy reaction to justify these natural inclinations towards what really seemed a craze or uncontrollable trend. ("Scruple—says the dictionary: a rough pebble in the shoe that hurts the foot.") Why, in effect, do they persist in making a sin out of something that is not one? Why be embarrassed about a taste, at worst, inocuous? With all the solemnness of his bearing, has Claudel not confessed, in the confusion of contemporary letters, that sometimes *The Three Musketeers* made him cry?[3]

The quote comes from "About the Detective Novel," written for a publishing group, *American Literary Agency,* in New York in July 1959 and printed one month later. This is one of three texts in which Reyes defends the genre; the other two are "Un gran policía de antaño," an imitation of François Vidocq, also written for the agency in September; and "Sobre la novela policial," published in the magazine *Todo* on 4 January 1945.

Reyes speaks of Robert L. Stevenson, Vidocq, Wilkie Collins, and Edgar Allan Poe. He executes a defense of *Edwin Drood* and advocates equipping this literature with classical rhetorical mechanisms going back to Homer and Sophocles. He never mentions Mexico's scanty national production; in fact, he ignores it.

Due to the dearth of critics who undertake to analyze the national art, its own writers have tackled the task: Xavier Villaurrutia wrote a prologue to *La obligación de asesinar* by Antonio Helú, and Jorge Ibargüengoitia wrote about James Bond and Agatha Christie in his weekly column in *Excélsior*. Paco Ignacio Taibo II, complaining about the lack of interest on the part of the reviewers, wrote an article for the Spanish magazine *Los Cuadernos del Norte* called "La (otra) novela policial" (1987), in which above and beyond discussing the work of contemporary Spaniards like Manuel Vázquez Montalbán, Eduardo Mendoza, Juan Madrid, and Andreu Martín, he claims that the Spanish product of the eighties is much superior to that of the English. Taibo II declares his belief that, though the critics ignore it, the genre continues to captivate the public. From that text comes the following quote:

> There is no doubt that detective fiction in Spanish enjoys very good health. If the work of experts weren't convincing enough, we would be obliged to add the attraction that the genre has exercised upon other authors who, without adopting it perhaps, have paid homage to it in at least one novel. Carlos Fuentes with *The Hydra Head*, Vicente Leñero with *Los albañiles*, Guillermo Thorndyke with *El caso Banchero*, Jorge Ibargüengoitia with *Dos crímenes* (Two Crimes) and in recent months, Mario Vargas Llosa with *Who Killed Palomino Molero?* The inclusion of writers who aren't genuine "detective writers" into the crime novel provides the reason why many believe that the techniques of the *noir* novel resonate so well on our continent.[4]

Although Reyes passes over the Mexican contributions, Carlos Monsiváis does not. In March 1973 he spoke at length, though still insufficiently, on the topic in an essay in the *Revista de la Universidad de México*, called "Ustedes que jamás han sido asesinados." It begins with a list of epigraphs by S. S. Van Dine, Agatha Christie, Dashiell Hammett, and Mickey Spillane, and the rest of the text is dedicated to a panoramic vision of the English and North American world, dedicating only an "Epilogue of Nationalist Intentions," a tenth of the whole, to a discussion of Mexican production. And his commentary is negative. He says:

> In general, the Mexican practice of police literature has been imitative, arbitrary and forced. Its cultivators seem few . . . and not overly convincing. My conclusion: In Mexico, it is not necessary, and nor does it seem probable, that a police novel or literature of espionage and intrigue should exist. The only suspense is that derived from self-consciousness. Will Demetrio Macías in *The Underdogs* ever manage to notice his role as a symbol of the Betrayed Revolution? Will Pedro Páramo ever understand that Comala is a village and a country and also human consciousness? Will the characters of Indio Fernández be able to figure out that they are just as picturesque but no more human than a postcard? These are the only Hitchcock-style queries which intrigue us. And the rest of our social and private lives refuses and rejects anything associated with intrigue or mystery.[5]

Monsiváis's statement is inaccurate. A suspenseful streak can certainly be found in *Pedro Páramo* or in the tales from *El llano en llamas* (The Burning Plain), as in "No Dogs Bark?" and "Tell Them Not to Kill Me!," and even in *The Underdogs*. The truth is, by the time the writer drafted these criticisms, there had already been a considerable contribution. The article was intended to provoke controversy, and it achieved it. María Elvira Bermúdez, one of the promoters of this type of literature in Mexico and the first to compile an anthology,[6] states in an interview (1981) with Francisco Torres, who read part of the Montsiváis quoted above: "I have to clarify: the authors who Carlos Monsiváis cites are exactly those who I include in my anthology *Los mejores cuentos policiacos mexicanos*. When he lectured about detective literature, many years ago, I was the clerk at the Supreme Court and he came to see me. He said that he was basing the lecture on an essay I had published in *El Nacional,* many years before. He even asked me for permission to use the essay. He said, very graciously: sometimes I cite you, but other times I don't. I told him, sure, go ahead."[7]

Bermúdez's introductory essay to her anthology (1955), based on texts and essays composed for *El Nacional,* was the first she had "seriously" written about the detective theme in Mexico. It had been preceded by a work of continental flavor by Anthony Boucher in *Publisher's Weekly* (1947),[8] which discussed the Latin American story in general, and was followed by several essays by Donald A. Yates, professor of literature at Michigan State University.[9] In fact, Yates published an article about the genre in Mexico in the *Kentucky Foreign Language Review* (1961), in which he speaks of Helú, Bermúdez, and Usigli, among others; moreover, he was the editor of another anthology, *El cuento policial latino-americano* (1964), a collection which includes stories by H. Bustos Domecq, Adolfo Pérez Zelachi, and Father Leonardo Castellani, along with three Mexicans—Bermúdez, Helú, and José Martínez de la Vega.[10] The dedication addressed Alfonso Reyes as a great man and a great humanist, a lifelong advocate of the detective genre. The following words, uttered only a few months before his death, might function just as well as an epigraph for this volume: 'A man's youth really ends and old age begins on the day that he loses his love for detective stories'."[11] Yates opens with an extensive prologue in which he comments on the total number of detective novels written in Latin America (about five hundred); he states that the three great centers of its creation are Buenos Aires, Mexico City and Santiago; and he goes on to discuss the work of Helú, Martínez de Vega, and Bermúdez.

Following the work of Monsiváis in chronological order, one finds a prologue to a second anthology by Torres himself, *El cuento policial mexicano,* the introduction of which includes commentaries about all the aforementioned critics. It brings together stories by Rafael Solana, Helú, Bermúdez, Martínez de la Vega, along with scarcely known veterans who collaborated in *Selecciones policiacas y de misterio* organized by Helú, among them Raymundo Quiroz Mendoza, Vincente Fé and Juan E. Closas. Moreover, it opens the door to new narrators, like Rafael Ramírez Heredia, though it ignores the contributions of Paco Ignacio Taibo II.

Torres also polemicizes about "Aquellos que jamás han sido asesinados":

> The "imitative" character of the works of the authors Monsiváis cites results from two circumstances: they are participating in an imported genre, so its first innovators had to begin by emulating masters and models. Moreover, we have already recalled that detective literature operates under a series of restrictions and schemata; the schematizing and reiteration are universal characteristics of the genre. . . . Maintaining that we lack the necessary cartesian mentalities for the genre, that our writers possess magical minds, couldn't possibly be a serious argument.[12]

Antonio Panells published another panoramic analysis of the genre in Latin America (1985),[13] which was followed by an essay by Eugenia Revueltas, "La novela policial en México y en Cuba."[14] In 1990, Amelia S. Simpson published a study about the production of the detective novel in Río de la Plata, Brazil, Cuba, and Mexico.

Although never with the desired depth and dedication, this study compares titles from different continental geographies and pauses to study each one with more patience than any previous work. She concludes: "The detective story in Mexico provides a larger sample for evaluation. A minor but nevertheless uninterrupted literary phenomenon since the twenties, the detective tale has not lacked an audience in Mexico, although, despite the contributions of prestigious figures such as Reyes and Usigli, the genre has acquired neither the status nor momentum it found from the forties on in Argentina."[15] Not quite true: The seventies and eighties would see a literary explosion of this "subgenre."

8

Antonio Helú

The cornerstone of detective letters in Mexico is Antonio Helú, born with the century and deceased in 1963. His first short stories began to appear in newspapers at the end of the twenties; one of them, "Pepe Vargas al teléfono," was published in 1929. Decades later they were compiled in *La obligación de asesinar,* a collection that was immediately included in *Queen's Quorum* by Ellery Queen, and thanks to which Helú entered the canon of Mexican detective writing. Moreover, in collaboration with Adolfo Fernández Bustamente, he wrote *El crimen de los Insurgentes,* a "detective comedy in three acts" published by the Distrito Federal's Editorial Teatro Mexicano Contemporáneo. He also selected, annotated, and wrote a prologue for an anthology, *El cuento enigmático,*[1] one of a collection of popular essays—a series called "La honda del espiritu," which includes contributions from the likes of Nathanial Hawthorne, Henry James, Poe, and Maupassant.

A naturalist with a passion for the description of places, customs and urban stereotypes, one of his first maneuvers as an author was to create various detectives which, by a process of distillation, narrowed down to only one, Máximo Roldán—part thieving rascal, part lucid unraveller of mysteries.[2] We never receive a concrete physical description of Roldán, although by turns he is described as thin, intelligent, and nervous. Roldán is the protagonist of *La obligación de asesinar,* divided into seven texts interconnected by references to objects or images. The setting, Mexico City, is urban. Roldán uses and abuses his intelligence; upon solving one mystery, he invariably dupes his fellow man and filches a portion of the loot for himself. He is blessed with *la verborrea,* the gift of gab. He incorporates the streetwise jargon of the era, making references to Porfirio Díaz, the state administration, along with popular folklore; in this way, he might be compared to Cantínflas, the popular vaudeville character created by Mario Moreno. Both characters utilize language in order to persuade and confuse, to elaborate

75

upon personal reality, and to oblige their fellow men to interact
with them on their own terms. For example, in "Piropos at mid-
night," one of the tales from the book which Yates included in his
anthology *El cuento policial latinoamericano,* Roldán discovers
three men committing a robbery and alerts two police officers. He
gives them a logical but hasty account of the crime, and as soon
as they outfit him with a baton and a gun, Roldán himself promptly
turns into a thief. Roldán, according to Amelia S. Simpson, "em-
bodies the hostility of the working class towards wealth and institu-
tional authorities."[3]

Therein lies the disquieting aspect of his personality. Although
he does solve cases by using his intellect, he always manages to
come out ahead. He boasts about his virtue, yet he frequently foils
the police and escapes punishment. Roldán therefore represents a
corrupt gentleman in the tradition of Arsène Lupin, simultaneously
for and against the law. And he doesn't merely steal; in the scenar-
ios into which Helú deposits Roldán, it suffices to point out the
guilty party without turning in the offenders. Roldán himself remains unpunished, forever at large. Helú's work thus defies the
traditional model of the detective text—in it, "good" does not always triumph over "evil."

By the sixth narrative in *La obligación de asesinar,* "Las tres
bolas de billar," Roldán acquires an assistant, Carlos Miranda, who
plays the role of a Doctor Watson. And in the last section, from
which the book takes its name, Miranda becomes the main character and Roldán disappears. In the same way, Helú introduces various detectives (Peter Vargas is another), and he has them strike
up conversations and even collaborate.

In 1946, Helú founded the magazine *Selecciones policiacas y de
misterio,* in which he published mostly well-known European and
North American authors, as well as Chileans, Argentines, Cubans,
and Mexicans like Rafael Bernal, Rafael Solana, José Martínez
de la Vega, and María Elvira Bermúdez. This publication further
solidified the genre in Mexico. Many writers first tested their luck
in it; some stayed with the magazine, like Vicente Alvarez and
Juan E. Closas, and never obtained fame independently, while
others most certainly did, like Juan Bustillo Oro. This Mexico City
native initiated his literary career in the magazine in 1934 and went
on, like so many others, to collaborate on *El Universal Ilustrado,*
the Sunday supplement of the newspaper by the same name, upon
which many detective writers have left their marks.[4]

Another one of these successful authors who went on to make

a career out of detective writing is Bermúdez. In her interview with Torres, she says:

> Thanks to Antonio Helú, many Mexican writers were able to fulfill their desires to write and to see detective stories published. Definitively he is the primordial figure for police literature in Mexico. There are some who say that Helú was not a good writer. Possibly he was not one of the best. Rafael Solana is better; Rafael Bernal, it goes without saying, is the greatest of them all. Antonio Helú did not subscribe to the classical detective genre. His was a hero, or better, an anti-hero, named Máximo Roldán, an emulation of Arsène Lupin; he cultivated the genre of the detective anti-novel (in the sense . . . of the friendly delinquent, good at heart, who robs the rich to help the poor), but not the classical detective tale, in the style of Agatha Christie, Ellery Queen, Simenon.[5]

In addition to his work on the magazine, Helú participated in the publishing house Editorial Novaro. Opening in the middle of the forties, the publishing house distributed various collections under the Nova-Mex label: "Escritores de América," "Cuentos y novelas," "Juvenil," "Aventuras y fantasía," and others. He served as a consultant for "Policiaca y de misterio." Various texts by Gaston Leroux—"The Bewitched Armchair," "The Bloody Doll," and "The Man Who Returned from The Beyond," among others— were adapted by Helú. *La obligación de asesinar* numbered 79 in the series and appeared in 1957. It was the first and only Mexican title. It cost $3.50 pesos and each of the 15,000 copies published, was accompanied by an anonymous inscription on the back cover, fabricated by Nova-Mex, which applauded the fact that the book had already been tranlsated into multiple languages. "The author of this series," it read, "can be termed, justly, a hero of the police novel. Not as an actor in the drama of mystery, blood, persecution and punishment, but for daring to cultivate a genre that seemed impossible in our literary environment, and for achieving his enterprise with dignity and success."

As previously stated, the edition featured a prologue by the notable dramaturgist and poet Xavier Villaurrutia, one of the members of the literary group *Los Contemporáneos* alongside his colleagues José Gorostiza, Gilberto Owen, and Salvador Novo, author of *La hidra* and *El yerro candante,* who died in 1950 at forty-seven. Villaurrutia assures readers that if he were a storyteller or a novelist he would write police novels. In addition, he asks more than once why Mexican writers have not developed their own detective novels and stories. "There exist, without a doubt," he says, "other reasons that are not merely based on the simple disdain with which it is generally viewed. To explain these reasons here would be lengthy and tedious. Moreover, it would be akin to stopping to contemplate a desert without noticing that there is a small oasis of stories by Antonio Helú to quench readers' thirst for detective fiction."[6]

A typical passage from *La obligación de asesinar* has Roldán committing a robbery. Note the following scene:

> It began to drizzle. The ground was flooding little by little, until it was completely covered with water. The rubber soles of his shoes made it difficult to walk. He slipped. With a great struggle he made it to the corner and gestured for a bus to stop. He groped for the bus, on his hands and knees, struggling to haul himself aboard. Noticing his posture and the difficulty with which he walked, the conductor and a passenger stretched out their hands, offering him support.
> "Do you feel sick, mister?"
> "No. Why?"
> "It's just that you're so pale, we thought . . . "
> Damnation! Would they be able to see what he had just done in his face?[7]

The last story, however, proves the most extensive—sixty-eight pages, in fact, long enough to be considered a short novel, an ad hoc genre for detective letters. It utilizes comic, discursive, and self-referential intermezzos, all of which clash with the rest of the narrative, which proceeds, for the most part, in a realistic, conventional manner. In the following passage, the omniscient narrator chats with the reader:

> The matter is already settled.
> It is well-known that in the Olympics there is still no Detective Competition. An event such as this could have very interesting results. For example, they might make bodies appear, killing off all of the champions of the various Olympic events: sprints, high jumps, shotput, discus and javelin, etc. Nothing would be lost, and one more event would be gained. And the crimes would be committed without a motive; or, indeed, the gold medal that adorns each one of the winners could serve as a motive. The purpose of the event would consist of discovering who committed the crimes. In the detective decathlon, the following individuals would compete: Sherlock Holmes, Nick Carter, Pep Rouletabille, Father Brown, Hercule Poirot, Philo Vance, Ellery Queen, Perry Mason, Nero Wolfe and all of the detectives that there have been in the world. And we would send Carlos Miranda, our hero, Mexican through and through, who takes nothing from his predecessors. And possibly we would have a world champion on our hands.[8]

The passage is valuable, not only for its ludicrous aspect, but because it lists some typical readings of the forties, all of which were quite common by the time Helú published his book. All of the detectives referred to above had appeared in the collection "Biblioteca de Oro," which suggests that Mexican readers were familiar with them in translation. The paragraph is also valuable for demonstrating the somewhat self-reducing impulse (though it aspires to the opposite) with which detective literature from Mexico entered onto the international scene.

The fact that Roldán was part-sleuth, part-thief fascinated the public, perhaps because he exhibited a Robin Hood-type nature and personified the intense distrust of the omnipotent police forces typical of the time. Such ideological connotations make him a symbol of class struggle. Helú, then, in addition to having inspired innumerable authors, was a promoter of "the Mexican" in the police novel—a model to imitate.

9
Rodolfo Usigli

THERE is a debate surrounding *Ensayo de un crimen,* a 1944 novel by Rodolfo Usigli (1905–79). Some, like Amelia S. Simpson, consider it "Mexico's first detective novel,"[1] while Bermudez, in his interview with Torres, says: "A stupendous novel, yes, but it is not strictly a detective novel. I admire it; it is considered a prototype of the Mexican police novel. I do not wish to detract from its literary merits, but it is not a classical police novel, about investigation, about mystery. I would term it criminological. Usigli owes his much-deserved fame to his work in theater, at which he is a master."[2]

Certainly Usigli is better known for *Corona de sombra* (Crown of Shadows, 1943), a historical drama similar in theme to *Noticias del Imperio,* Fernando del Paso's third novel, about what would have happened if the Empress Carlota, after losing her mind, had recovered her wits and had recorded the adventures of her and her husband Maximiliano de Habsburgo.

In addition, there is *El gesticulador* (1937), which examines how lies and myths contribute to the national personality. César Rubio is a French university professor who shares the same name as a missing revolutionary general. When an American investigator who is conducting research about Rubio (the soldier) approaches Rubio (the professor), a case of mistaken identity ensues; the professor plays along and pretends to be his alter ego. His luck changes overnight and he becomes a presidential candidate. But he is assassinated, and a few years later, his son unsuccessfully attempts to prove that Rubio was not actually Rubio.

Usigli taught Ibargüengoitia in the Department of Philosophy and Letters in the Universidad Nacional Autónoma de México, and their literary legacies bear similarities. *Tres comedias impolíticas* (1933–55) by the former writer, which includes *Noches de estío* and *El Presidente y el ideal,* ridiculed Mexican political lifestyles, corruption, and hypocrisy as much as the novels of his student,

Los relámpagos de agosto (The Lightning of August, 1964), *Maten al león* (1967), and *Los pasos de López* (1981).

Although his work abounds with satirical essays and assigned pieces, *Ensayo de un crimen* is Usigli's only novel. Its protagonist is Roberto de la Cruz, a dandy who aspires to commit an aesthetically perfect crime. This interest in the smug, ridiculous bourgeois is a hallmark trait of the forties, as Mexico struggled through the petroleum conflict and the world was embroiled in global war. The caprice of Usigli's work shows itself as he dedicates three hundred-plus pages to a series of platonic crimes in a setting in which one kills for love, ideology, money, or jealousy but seldom for beauty.

Moreover, what the writer leaves out is as important as what he includes. The nation enters a period of intense patriotism and one of its thousand financial jolts, but none of this bothered de la Cruz, who lived as if in a glass bubble, isolated and egomaniacal. He suffers, hates, and hatches plans that are unacceptable and ridiculous, or kind-hearted and humanitarian, in a city that might be St. Petersburg or London just as well as Mexico. These references are not idle; although the writer was a confessed admirer of George Bernard Shaw, the inspiration for *Ensayo de un crimen* came from Dostoevsky's *Crime and Punishment* and from Thomas De Quincey, especially "On Murder Considered as One of the Fine Arts."

De la Cruz lives possessed by an interior force that is brutal and persecutes him daily without respite. His attacks begin when he hears "The Red Prince," a waltz by Waldteufel that had been the tune of a music box he had owned in his childhood. The waltz causes him to lose his wits, contort, and feel compelled to end the lives of people nearby. He neither robs nor rapes them (two of his victims are women, the third a homosexual); he murders to achieve his aim of scouring his fellow men clean of disagreeable "types," the undesirables abhorrent to society at large, a subpopulation he and only he can eliminate. In this way, de la Cruz is similar to Raskolnikov, because he murders with humanity in mind. The character also pays tribute to De Quincey, because blood nauseates him and he abhors violence, yet, like a good antinomian, he believes that murder is on some level one of the modalities of good.

And now, a series of details which contribute to the suspense: He opens the novel with de la Cruz shaving himself with boiling water and a sharp razor. Suddenly, he feels as if his throat had been slit, and he breaks into a cold sweat. We know little about his past, only about the present. He is at the most forty-five years old. His malady impels him to incessantly mutter aloud the

phrases, "Where do all the dead go, sir? Where do they go?" He
must murder and he cannot control himself. In the interview with
Torres, Bermúdez says that Usigli "based *Ensayo de un crimen* on
a real incident. The events occurred on Yucatán Street, in a house
that still exists."[3]

Roberto de la Cruz's first victim is supposed to be the unpleas-
ant, affluent Patricia Terrazas. He plans the crime in thirty precise
steps, but as he approaches Yucatán No. 48, the residence of the
soon-to-be corpse, he realizes that someone has beaten him to it.
He does not know who, and nor do we. He sees an apelike silhou-
ette (an obvious homage to Poe) with a camera leaving the mansion, and thinks that it belongs to his usurper. A profound grief
seizes him: He had come to kill, and yet he could not achieve his
aim. He promptly decides that it was his murder, his and no one
else's, and he leaves his fingerprints everywhere. Soon he is locked
up in a penitentiary only to be absolved of the crime shortly thereafter. Again he attempts a similar exploit, now against another
dandy; and a third, against one of his lovers. In the customary
fashion, his deeds are ultimately exposed thanks to the investigations of the ex–inspector Herrera, a ghostly presence who plays
the role of *deus absconditus:* He appears before de la Cruz on the
most unexpected occasions, warns him when danger is near and
investigates without interfering.

The presence of Herrera is one major strike against Bermúdez'
argument that *Ensayo de un crimen* is not a detective novel. If the
tale is indeed told from the point of view of Roberto de la Cruz,
the ex–inspector's aparition is a reminder of the justice and order
which haunt the protagonist. There is no genuine deduction and
no one is responsible for deciphering secrets; and the author does
not permit his readers to know biographical details about the criminal (nor those of the ex–inspector) from the start. *Ensayo de un
crimen,* then, like the adventures of Fantomas, is a detective novel
told from the perspective of the delinquent.

Similar to what occurs with Máximo Roldán, de la Cruz, although he spends a few months in jail, he does it for the first crime,
one he never committed. Even after he commits other murders,
he remains unpunished. This is one of the dialogues that de la Cruz
sustains with Herrera near the end of the novel, upon discovering
the death of the beautiful Nena Cervantes, spouse of de la Cruz.
He kills her on an aesthetic impulse; the newspapers accuse him
of having robbed a life on account of jealousy, since de la Cruz
knew that she had a lover:

"I have studied this point," responded the Inspector, after exchanging a wide smile with the Chief of Investigations, "and some psychiatric specialists tell me that it has to do with a complex of . . . well, of something, that shows up in very jealous men. They couch their acts of jealousy in all pretexts imaginable in order to convince themselves that they do not respond to jealousy, that they are not jealous men. Your crime is a most savage crime of passion, that is certain, but it is among the more basic of those committed of late in Mexico, Mr. De la Cruz."

Roberto de la Cruz rose violently from his chair, slapped the Inspector's table, and with a whistling, stifled voice on account of his bad nervous respiration, confessed to everything. From the beginning he yearned to commit the most gratuitous and the most Mexican of crimes. He wanted to murder Patricia Terrazas without the slightest motive, and on seeing that someone had beaten him to it, he had diverted suspicions towards himself. But that was not all. He had killed Count Schartzemberg with the same lack of motive. He feverishly recounted the details, possessed like an artist or a sage who explains the miracle of creation or the science of transformation; he related his system of calculation and experimentation, everything, in the end, that had occupied the mechanisms of his life and thoughts during the past year. He left out only one thing: his childhood trauma and the peculiar effect the music, *The Red Prince,* exerted upon him. He kept this to himself, in the midst of his excitement, because he had an exceedingly clear premonition that in men there are things that must never be passed from one to another. His declarations were dizzily typed, and, observing his passion, the two officials stopped smiling. When Roberto de la Cruz had finished, the Inspector of Police offered him a cigarette, patted him on the shoulder and accompanied him personally to his cell.[4]

Disturbingly enough, the protagonist's assertions, which he has kept secret throughout the entire book, are not taken seriously. To the end, de la Cruz goes unpunished. He remains free but unsatisfied. Usigli's message is clear; in a country full of disguises and hypocrisy, not even a confessed criminal gets what he deserves; nothing can be crystalline, everything perverts, corrupts, and twists the truth out of shape. The aesthetic crime of de la Cruz is not a crime at all in a setting where the aesthetic has no place.

Luis Buñuel made a cinematic adaptation of *Ensayo de un crimen* in 1955. The movie departs from the original plot. During the upsurge of the new surrealism, elements of *roman à clef* began to lose their appeal. According to rumors, the adaptation was supposed to have been by Usigli and Buñuel together, but the two separated after an altercation and it was finished by a friend of the director. On seeing the final product, Usigli complained to the syndicate, but nothing came of it because the disclaimer had read "inspirada en . . ."—"inspired by." (The screenplay of the movie is by Buñuel and Eduardo Ugarte). In fact, the Spanish director changed the title of the foreign version to *La vida criminal de Archibaldo de la Cruz;* in other words, he changed the name of the protagonist (played by Ernesto Alonso). He changed other things, too: de la Cruz, for example, dreams of killing three women (Adriana Welter, Miroslava, and Rita Macedo); the presence of mannequins in the film creates a fertile ground for fetishism.[5]

In Usigli's version, the strong emotions of the antihero force him to seize upon a life purpose and destiny, a raison d'être. He lives alone in a room rented in a hotel. His activities are artificial and guided by compulsions similar to those felt by the creatures of Proust. When we encounter him, he is perpetually drinking brandy or a highball, or playing poker with diplomatic friends. He also appears dining in elegant restaurants, going to Cuernavaca and Acapulco, thumbing through Bécquer's *Rimas,* or smoking one of his Lucky Strikes. Robert Louis Stevenson, in his astonishing *The Wrecker,* written in collaboration with his stepson Lloyd Osburne in 1892, admits what has already been said in chapter 3, that the characters in a detective novel run the risk of ending up mere cogs in a mechanism that continually upstages them. Nothing of this type happens in *Ensayo de un crimen.* There are, of course, artificial scenes; in one, the antihero slits his own veins with no apparent motive; in another there is an automobile accident, included only to eliminate a superfluous character. The detailed, knowledgeable descriptions of Mexico City, from the elite perspective and not the popular—that is, making no allusions to the thousand alleyways and prestigious cafés, the hang-outs and newspaper stands—are the passages in which Usigli proves his expertise. Taking into consideration his economics and his interests, as well as his aristocratic aesthetic passions, Usigli is the antithesis of his compatriot Juan Rulfo, whose characters are plagued with bad luck and engage in an unbalanced battle with adversity.

Though it is narrated from the point of view of the criminal, *Ensayo de un crimen* may be the finest detective novel ever written in Mexico.

10

Rafael Solana

RAFAEL Solana (1914–91), another writer who began his literary career as an editor of *El Universal Ilustrado,* worked there until 1944 before going on to run magazines of widespread importance like *Letras de México* and *Taller poético.* A prolific poet, novelist, critic, cinematic screenwriter and journalist,[1] Solana published only one detective story, "El crimen de tres bandas," which appeared one year after *Ensayo de un crimen* in the collection "Lunes" (1945) with a prologue by Henrique González Casanova. According to Vicente Francisco Torres, editor of the anthology *El cuento policial mexicano,* which featured it as the first story in the collection, the text "is one of the best detective works written in our country."[2] The praise is rather too high. Certainly, it is a story at once brief, sober, precise, detailed, and polished; at times, however, it seems too mechanical, like clockwork fine-tuned to such a degree that it exists apart from humanism.

An anonymous narrator mediates the text in first person, in the form of a diary. The masculine voice is that of a friend of Eduardo Murrieta, with whom he plays pool and chess and frequently discusses war-related topics (the story takes place at the end of World War II, closer to 1945), movie premieres, bullfights, politics, and boxing matches. By means of the diary entries, we soon discover that Murrieta has resolved to kill his wife, who has been unfaithful, and his boss, her lover. They will effect the murder scheme through a remote control apparatus installed in an apartment on Amsterdam Street, the lovers' trysting place; upon entering the room, a gun will fire at one of the two, and then a large sack of lime will finish the job by crushing the victim.

Seen from a distance, these stratagies seem predictable and simple; they aren't when the reader approaches them for the very first time. After Murrieta commits the crime on the precise date and at the precise time, for a few moments we lack sufficient information and we question who has fallen victim. The narrator suspects is was Murrieta himself, which precipitates the unease of the lovers and spurs them to commit suicide. The narrator is stricken with grief and mourns his friend. The story ends with a meeting between the narrator and a transformed Murrieta, one year later, no longer in Mexico City, where the majority of the action took place, but in Costa Rica. The criminal explains he had hired an unwitting laborer, similar in appearance to himself, to serve as a victim. When the limestone fell, the look-alike caused his confidant to suspect that it was Murrieta who had perished in the place of one of the two lovers.

March 29:
If I believed in apparitions, my hair would have stood on end tonight, when I saw a corpse come to life. The suffocating heat of the night had me drinking a little more whisky than I'm used to; maybe that kept me cool when, approaching the pool table in a casino in San José, Costa Rica, I recognized a friend of mine who I had believed had died under tragic circumstances in Mexico, approximately a year ago. He was much paler, had grown a black, pointed mustache that exaggerated the pallor of his skin, and had two black sideburns that also stood out against his face; some blue glasses and a white linen suit, topped off with a Panama hat, gave the finishing touches to his new personality; but I recognized him instantly by the firmness, precision, and prodigious creativity with which he shot a three-banded carom.[3]

During his exile in Central America, Murrieta proceeds to explain the intricacies of his deeds. Again, as in the cases of Máximo Roldán and Roberto de la Cruz, he manages to commit his offense without undergoing judgment by the law. It begins to seem as if, in the Mexican detective novel, it is sufficient to confess a crime, punishment notwithstanding. In the work of Paco Ignacio Taibo II, this sort of immunity is brought to its extreme.

Solana emulates the "classical" model, in the tradition of British writers like Dorothy L. Sayers, Agatha Christie, and Arthur Conan Doyle. His middle-class characters do not have distinctive Mexican characteristics. They speak in an educated language, they dress like Latin American citizens, their style is cosmopolitan and sophisticated—they play billiards, drink whisky, and keep their lovers in the lap of luxury. In contrast to Usigli's novel, in "El crimen de tres bandas" there is a detailed process of investigation, and there is a distinct desire for the truth to reign over the chaos, though no detective figure exists. That is to say, the elements of the formula that do *not* appear are the triumph of good over evil and the presence of a rational investigator. Even so, because the deductions occur with the aid of dated diary entries and a narrator, the story fits the genre, especially because the conclusion sees the emergence of the truth.

11

José Martínez de la Vega

Perhaps the most humorous and idiosyncratic author, and the most "Mexican" of this literary firmament of detective fiction, is José Martínez de la Vega (1908–54). In addition to his chronicles of the Revolution and his comic texts, his repertoire includes two collections of short stories, *Humorismo en camiseta* (1946), and six years later, *Péter Pérez, detective de Peralvillo y anexas,* in which he utilizes the detective formula to cultivate his strong sense of irony.[1]

In the second collection, an epigraph appears even before the title: "I was in the Department of Public Education and someone said, 'Propriety is a rip-off.' I exclaimed, 'Well, I haven't touched it! Go ahead and search me.' And then they found this book." From then on, everything is a joke, satirizing the political and social life of the nation. In the forties, Peralvillo was usually one of the poorest neighborhoods in Mexico City, in which vendors wandered the streets and illicit transactions were carried out. Police raids, arrests, and prosecutions occurred with frequency, even though the gendarmes and bailiffs were apprehensive about venturing into the district. Even suggesting that the protagonist is a Peralvillo detective is a joke from the start; "anexas," used like a suffix, is lower-class slang for "the surroundings."

Péter Pérez sleeps on matting with a board for a pillow; he has a telephone but he can't pay for it; he frequently disguises himself with a costume beard, like Valente Quintana; and he has a pipe and a tiny hat. He doesn't steal and he doesn't lie. He is a typical anachronism, symbolic of honesty and good sense, a man of a tradition who cares little for money. A prologue by Miguel Ángel Ceballos to the 1952 edition of *Péter Pérez* reads:

> In a social surround as corrupt as ours, where so many lie, and cheat, and steal, and malinger, and masquerade, and are avid for pleasure and have discarded all moral decency . . . Péter Pérez, who is industrious, who is honest, who fulfills his mission, who respects the letter of the

law, who is faithful to his duties . . . can only be viewed as someone maladapted to his environment, that is to say, as a greatly comic, absurd character, at whom we can do little but laugh.[2]

His adventures are simple and brief (between five and ten pages). They have provocative titles, which invite mockery: "El misterio del indio redimido," "La triste muerte del juez rural," "El caso del millonario bostezante" and "El secreto de la lata de sardinas."

Péter Pérez has an opponent. He is not precisely an Inspector Javert, but rather a caricature of the constables who precede Sherlock Holmes in cases which they never close. His name: Sergeant Juan Vélez, who calls upon Detective Peralvillo to solve mysteries he can't crack. Peralvillo operates by means of intellect, deductive logic, and above all, sarcastic mechanisms through which he criticizes the Partido Revolucionario Institucional, diplomatic corruption, the failure of laws for public protection, thereby revealing national farce. The following exchange comes from the interview with Bermúdez: "By reading the works of Pepe Martínez de la Vega and your own, we see that detective stories contain social criticism," states Torres. The novelist responds, "Of course, although that isn't their fundamental purpose. Novels, stories, as well as theatrical productions, always contain social criticism. Above all else, Pepe Martínez de la Vega is a great comedian."[3]

In "El misterio del indio redimido," for example, the body of a native appears in a small village in the Republic, near the capital. The town inspector decides that the intoxicated Indian had drunk himself to death, but Péter Pérez discovers, to everyone's surprise, that Don German (the supposed Indian) was in fact a politician in disguise who had openly supported the PRI in the municipal elections and had been murdered by one of the locals. Martínez de la Vega suggests that polititians lie to villagers and that Don German had died at the hands of a discontented soldier—that, in fact, he deserved everything he got.

Humor and criticism of the legal system are also devices used by Argentines Jorge Luis Borges and Adolfo Bioy Casares, who under the pseudonyms H. Bustos Domecq and Suárez Lynch jointly published *Six Problems for Don Isidro Parodi* and *Un modelo para la muerte* (A Model for Death, 1946). The parodic attitude starts with the name of the detective—Parodi—and carries on through the rest of the text. Writers have developed a satire called Armchair Detective, in which an investigator solves mysteries intellectually without much physical exertion.

Parodi demonstrates the same corporal limitation, but his is not

voluntary: He is in jail, having committed the indiscretion of rent-
ing a room to a clerk who was more than a year overdue in his rent.
The vernacular of the stories resorts to plays on words, criticism of
the populism of Juan Domingo Perón, a hot item during this time
in Argentina. Martínez de la Vega effects a similarly skillful narrative. His private eye is free, but law and money are not on his side.
Péter Pérez spoofs grand detective exploits through his own down-
to-earth antics and antigovernment commentaries.

Donald A. Yates says:

> Authors of detective literature can express their lack of confidence
> in fundamental principles of justice in a variety of ways. One of these
> consists of mocking the rigorous rules which traditionally restrict the
> structure of police fiction. (This reveals itself largely in the detective
> literature written by Argentines.) This irreverent attitude can surface
> in the comic stories of Mexican José Martínez de la Vega. His capri-
> cious vision of the classical mystery of the "locked door" presents the
> problem of a body that appears in a completely enclosed room. The
> crime baffles the world until the comic detective Péter Pérez shows
> authorities that the room was indeed effectively closed, except for a
> certain detail that had escaped them: The room lacked a roof![4]

The story to which Yates refers is the eleventh in "Péter Pérez,
detective de Peralvillo y anexas,"[5] the tales of which are narrated
in the third person, are enjoyable, not sophisticated in the least,
and appeal to the masses, thus appearing in newspapers in the
capital. Like all comedy, stereotypes are common: inept cops, stut-
terers, ridiculous servants, cinema directors with berets and cigars.
Moreover, one must add that such was the success of the volume
that the author converted some of the stories into radio programs,
produced for The Sidney Ross Co., as he explains in his "Essay
on Mexican Comedy".[6]

Péter Pérez is an observer who disregards and rebels against
the established order. He is a member of the lower classes whose
consciousness does not oblige him to compete with the rich. While
investigating his cases, once in a while he sent a starving wretch
to jail, handing him over to Sergeant Juan Vélez without exhibiting
the slightest pang of remorse.

12

María Elvira Bermúdez

AFTER Helú, María Elvira Bermúdez has done more than anyone else for the genre in Mexico.

She was born in Durango in 1916 and died in Mexico City in 1987. A lawyer, prolific literary critic, storyteller, and novelist, she is the author of a variety of collections, among them her narrative *Detente sombra,* (1984) inspired in some poetic passages by Sor Juana Inés de la Cruz.[1] Beginning in the fifties, she started to publish her work in *El Nacional,* which includes substantial commentaries and apologias on detective fiction and studies of (among others) Helú, Paco Ignacio Taibo II and Rafael Bernal.[2] Moreover, she has written multiple prologues for the collection *Sepan cuantos . . .* by Porrua. This includes works like *Tales of the Grotesque and Arabesque* by Edgar Allan Poe, *Captain Thunder* by Emilio Salgari, and *Michael Strogoff* by Jules Verne.[3]

Three of her detective works stand out: her 1955 anthology; *Diferentes razones tiene la muerte,*[4] an undated novel; and a collection of stories, *Muerte a la zaga* (1986).[5] Her first story appeared in 1948, published by Helú in *Selecciones de crimen y de misterio.*

Like Helú and Martínez de la Vega, Bermúdez speaks through her own detective, an honest, astute journalist, Armando H. Zozaya. He appears in two of the titles above. In *Diferentes razones tiene la muerte,* she describes him in the following manner:

> He was around 30 years old, probably more. He was a little taller than average and at a first look he could pass unnoticed. With a second glance, though, his image fixes indefinitely in the memory of those who know his distinguished demeanor, his strange mix of agility and indolence; the sultry, playful mouth shadowed over by a small but aggressive brown mustache; green eyes, sardonic and inquisitive to others but curiously sad in his moments of privacy.[6]

The adventures in which he appears are standard. The setting, however, is intrinsically Mexican: a village in Coyoacán, a street in the Roma colony, the countryside, and so on. Zozaya speaks little but properly, neither cracking jokes nor abusing the language. He explains his deductions like Poirot: without showing off, soberly, never exploiting his position of authority.

In *Diferentes razones* Georgina Llorente, the widow of Prado, invites a series of guests to her estate in Coyoacán, all of whom are related in one manner or another to the deceased. Some resist, but ultimately all attend the gathering. During their visit, there are two consecutive murders: one of Mario Ortiz, age forty-eight, Georgina's ex-husband; and the other of Diana Leech y García, a Yankee friend of the hostess. They call the police to investigate, but when the official sleuths fail to produce a murderer, Armando H. Zozaya, thirty-one, takes the case at the invitation of Georgina's stepson, Miguel Prado. In the end, Zozaya solves the mystery, uncovering the truth slowly and methodically by studying clues and fingerprints.

"Cabos sueltos," the third story in *Muerte a la zaga*, depicts Zozaya in a similar situation: a murder by poisoning during a party in Durango. After his investigation, the detective concludes that a certain Tito is the perpetrator. The same formulaic structure repeats itself in the rest of the stories, which are always conventional, never innovative.

"El embrollo del reloj," which appeared in volume 67 of the magazine and in the anthologies by Yates and Torres, reunites Zozaya and Miguel Prado, the lawyer who first introduces us to the detective in *Diferentes razones*. It differs from the previous stories, though, because it is set among the poorer classes. Juan García, a humble laborer, is accused of killing his sister-in-law Rosa while her sister and daughter are away at the market. This possibility seems likely, because among García's possessions is a watch, shattered and stopped at 11:45, the precise time of the crime. Here and there various colloquial idiosyncracies appear in the speech of the lower classes: *ahí nomás, reló, amuinada, compa,* and so on. In the end, his deductions lead him to Ismael Flores, who was enamored of Rosa but whose advances were rejected. He unfolds the mystery before a panel of corrupt governmental officials. Torres says that the story "shows not only that the detective story can happen among humble people, but that a lack of honorability among police authorities is no obstacle to literature of this type."[7]

In her interview with Torres, Bermúdez establishes a hierarchy of four types of detective novel:

a) The police novel proper, that is to say, the classic in which a detective acts and in which the principle problem is, "Who is the murderer?"
b) The criminological story, which narrates the perpetration of a crime from the point of view of the criminal; *Ensayo de un crimen* is the archetype of this variant. It is for this reason I do not classify it as detective fiction precisely, but rather, as a criminological novel.
c) The mystery story, which is a more complex and varied genre.
d) The horror story, the lineage of which goes back as far as the gothic novel; for example, *The Castle of Otranto.* [8]

The six stories that comprise *Muerte a la zaga* appeared in *El Nacional* starting in the sixties; likewise for those in *Diferentes razones.* All of these fit tidily into the first category above. Bermúdez writes Zozaya, Prado, and the rest of her characters into classical stories which emulate the British model; the detective, hardly intrepid at a physical level, is a heavyweight in wrestling matches of the intellect.

Reading Bermúdez's texts is never satisfactory; they convey the impression that all is premeditated, and the characters are dull and mechanical. In addition, her reviews and commentaries suffer from a lack of critical rigorousness. Hers is the work of an amateur, the pastime of a judge in the Mexico City Supreme Court of Justice, the product of patient and selfless readings, and of the courage to try her own hand. In the aforementioned essay "La (otra) novela policiaca," based on a lecture given at Northwestern University in Illinois, Paco Ignacio Taibo II does not even mention her. [9]

It is disturbing that Bermúdez would be the only woman who participates in this literary trend. Why? One must present several answers: The few feminine quills in the display case of Mexican narratives, apart from some exceptions (Sor Juana, Antonieta Rivas Mercado, Inés Arredondo, Elena Garro), owe their places to changes effected by the 1968 movement in Tlatelolco. Suddenly voices have been raised whose principle interest has been clearing an *arrebatado* (enraged, passionate) space for *lo femenino.* [10] Figures like Elena Poniatowska, Angeles Mastretta, Carmen Boullosa, Angelina Muñiz-Huberman, María Luisa Puga, and Luisa Josefina Hernández emerged with a unique perspective but were never attracted to literary subgenres. Their work is political by nature, though their themes need not always bear ideological attributes.

Bermúdez does not belong to this faction, but rather, to its antecedent. She cannot be seen as a precursor because her work demonstrates interests that never attracted the post-Tlatelolco novelists. Nor does she introduce the militant tone of the feminist

voice into detective letters. In fact, she might even be compared to
Agatha Christie and her Hercule Poirot (but not her Miss Marple!):
Zozaya is a man; his witnesses and victims are just as likely to be
men or women. It is curious that Bermúdez did not create a feminine detective. She would have been the first of her kind in Mexico!
Why did she choose not to do so? Because of the limitations that
restrained women in the society of her time, which would have
made such a character implausible? This cannot be the answer,
because Martínez de la Vega's Péter Pérez is a wretch and Helú's
Máximo Roldán is a thief. As these characters confirm, detectives,
in Mexico, have frequently sprung from marginalized sectors. The
answer, then, must be the author's lack of knowledge of the limits
and possibilities of the literary subgenre.

13

Rafael Bernal

T_{AIBO} II says:

> It is difficult to know who started the flood . . . In Mexico it may be *El complot mongol,* by Rafael Bernal (an absolutely accidental novel, but without a doubt a part of this new trend) and edited in 1969, which passed through book stores with neither shame nor glory.[1]

If indeed *Ensayo de un crimen,* as he said, is considered by some to be the first detective novel in Mexico, others—like Bermúdez and Taibo II—dismiss it on account of its evident shortage of formulaic elements. They counter, for their part, with this novel by Rafael Bernal, *El complot mongol,* and they elevate it to a sort of beacon or foundation.

As we shall see, the book belongs to the third category in our typology described in chapter one: the espionage novel. Before examining it, it is worthwhile to present some facts about the author.

Rafael Bernal was born in Morelia, Michoacán, in 1915, and died in Switzerland in 1972. As a youthful sinarquista, he underwent numerous incarcerations and exiles. He was a reclusive writer who experimented with poetry, television, and theater, and became famous for his stories and novels. He enjoyed traveling and dedicated a large part of his life to globe-trotting, and settled in various locations, from the United States to the Orient, from Europe to the Philippines. In his prime he served as a diplomat, which distanced him from his native Mexico. He collaborated to produce newspapers and magazines, both national and foreign. His literary ambitions were manifest in the subjects he addressed: social and historical order as well as entertainment. In other words, he was a skillful storyteller and used fables to explore the human condition.

The novel which exemplifies his social concerns is *Memorias de Santiago Oxtotipan,* published in 1945. It discusses the Revolution and its regressive progress, and it weighs the pros and cons of a national reality that so obstinately resists change. *Su nombre era muerte* is a sort of *Robinson Crusoe;* it is a 1947 novel about an individual who lives on the distant shores of Usumacinta, far from the vices of humanity yet mounting an internal defense against his own primal passions. Another one of his books takes place in the jungles of the Orinoco and Caracas.[2]

He also wrote *Trópico* (1946), a collection of short stories, the most celebrated of which is "La media hora de Sebastian Constantino." Its protagonist is a thug nicknamed "Forty-Five" who enters a bar to eliminate his foe. The beauty of the narrative lies in its imitative borrowing of the techniques of Dos Passos and Hemingway in "The Killers"—which depicts a violent scene of surprising similarity. In addition, Bernal toys with a dichotomy between internal and external time, a theme in vogue at that time thanks to the philosophies of Henri Bergson. In real, collective time, only seconds transpire between the moment that Sebastian Constantino enters the bar to the instant that shots are fired; the relative time experienced by Constantino is years or even decades, an ample enough interlude for the hero to contemplate his past. The same device already had been immortalized by Borges in "El milagro secreto" (The Secret Miracle), and before that by Ambrose Bierce in "An Occurrence at Owl Creek Bridge." All three are atemporal tales of crime and suspense with surprise endings.

In 1967 the writer published another collection of brief narratives, the lighthearted *En diferentes mundos* dedicated to Agustin Yáñez.[3] The collection includes several notable stories, among them "El alacrán," a tribute to Hawthorne and Bierce. It is about identity, the struggle for power during the Revolution, and, more manifestly, how a fatal practical joke is ultimately not very funny. There are two protagonists: Colonel García, who is on the verge of shooting Jacobito; the former has accused the latter of being the fearsome bandit, The Scorpion. The characters undergo a sudden juxtaposition of personalities.

El complot mongol, a novel written two years earlier, was an antecedent of *The Hydra Head* by Carlos Fuentes. If one were to read the books out of their chronological order, Filiberto García, Bernal's hero, would seem to recall Felix Maldonado, Fuentes' bureaucratic detective who works for the secretary of Industrial Development. Both men are womanizers; both stumble upon conspiracies which threaten to destabilize Mexico—Maldonado collaborates with Americans and Israelis against the Arabs, García prevents a delayed Maoist revolution in Cuba and the possible assassination of the U.S. president. One difference, however, is that the first detective is highly intellectual and the second is not; in fact, we know very little about García's past while it is well known that Maldonado pursued studies in New York at Columbia University, and that he and his boss exchange passwords culled from Shakespeare.

Filiberto García is a scoundral who has killed a handful of times; he extracts enjoyment from hurting his fellow man; he uses Yardley cologne; he polishes his .45 with a chamois and always carries it with him in the pocket of his slacks; he is clumsy and foolish, and he kills for pleasure against the orders of his superiors; moreover, he is incapable of forming a thought of any great depth.

Bernal uses a vulgar language punctuated with insults, an innovation that would later become the model for Taibo II in the adventures of his private eye, Héctor Belascoarán Shayne. In fact, the novel as a whole is a sort of template for Taibo II; he sketches a literary map of Mexico City, not from the aesthetic perspective of Fuentes in *Where the Air Is Clear,* but on the level of a rubbish heap, a cesspool of violence, drugs, blood, and crime. The metropolises of *An Easy Thing* or *Regreso a la misma ciudad y bajo la lluvia* by Taibo II reflect the same interest: he delves deeply into the farthest reaches of debased and miserable lives.

Bernal also maneuvers to demonstrate how the military legacy of the Revolution left a high concentration of well-paid murderers and displaced thugs roaming the humanity-infested streets. Take as a case in point the following paragraph, in which the writer interweaves a third-person narrative, an omniscient voice and Filiberto García's stream of consciousness:

> The night invaded in grays, muddying the streets of Luis Moya, and the traffic, as usual at that hour, was intolerable. He resolved to go on foot. The Colonel had met him at seven. He had time. He walked toward Avenida Juárez and turned to the left, towards the Caballito. He could go slowly. He had time. All of my damned life I've had time. Killing is not a very time-consuming profession, especially now that we're learning all about law, order and government. During the Revolution it had been another thing altogether, but then I was just a kid. An assistant to my General Marchena, one of so many generals, second-rate. A cute little lawyer from Saltillo said that he was a money-grubbing general, but that little lawyer is dead now. I don't like jokes like that. Dirty stories are fine, but as far as jokes go, you have to know how to respect other people, you have to know how to respect Filiberto García and his generals. Damn those jokes![4]

There is no doubt that *El complot mongol* is a xenophobic, racist text. The enemy is an Asian minority from the capital; he is assaulted and verbally attacked. Such a maneuver, one might deduce, both entertains Bernal and makes his agent even more distinctively Mexican in a country where sentiments toward immigrants are negative.

Contrary to Taibo II's statements above, the book met with immediate success when it hit the shelves and was reprinted in three editions. It is, however, prone to a combination of overwhelming simplicity and insufficient lyricism. Bernal produces too many bodies and only a minimal dosage of sex. It is useful to compare the novel with works from the same time period by Gustavo Sáinz and José Agustín. Bernal falls at the opposite extreme of the spectrum: he is a confirmed conservative and an ineloquent writer. The opening paragraph from chapter 2 proves the former point:

> Mexico, with a certain hesitancy, calls Dolores Street its Chinatown. It is a neighborhood of only one street with old houses, with one pathetic alleyway dying for a mystery. There are shops smelling of Canton and Fukien, a few restaurants. But everything lacks the warmth, lights and pennants, lanterns and the atmosphere one observes in other Chinatowns, like in San Francisco or Manila. Rather than a Chinatown, it gives an impression of an old street where some Chinese have anchored themselves, orphans of imperial dragons and mysterious, thousand-year-old potions.[5]

Another example of Bernal's style and preferred themes occurs in *Un muerto en la tumba*. Here the protagonist is Don Teódulo Batanes, a priest inspired by G. K. Chesterton's Father Brown and with whom Bernal introduced the religious detective into the fabric of Mexican police fiction.

This book also capitalizes upon the mystery of the locked room: The action unfolds in a tomb at Monte Albán, Oaxaca. After centuries of remaining sealed, the vault is suddenly opened by a group of archaeologists and political officials, along with Don Teódulo. Everyone is shocked when they discover a still-warm body inside.

Batanes appears in numerous tales, always demonstrating the same characteristics: he is an old cleric, intelligent; he is never welcome among the high ranks of the police; he has a passion for archaeology and has an irritating habit of doubling words; that is, he makes excessive use of synonyms. In the following passage, don Teodulo deduces that the murder had been committed by Robles, a shady forty-year-old businessman who ransacks ruins and sells artifacts in the United States:

The first thing that caught my attention, when I found out that don Elpidio, may God rest his soul, had *died or perished* from a bruise on the back of his neck, produced by a steel or iron crowbar, was that flint *knife or blade* buried in his chest. We have been informed already by the *doctor or forensic scientist* that the death was instantaneous and that the blow to the neck was enough. Then what purpose did the knife serve, sunk a half hour after the presumed time of death? It would have to be the act of a *lunatic or a madman;* but, with a crime as well planned as this one, one cannot believe that it would have been committed by a mentally disturbed person. Therefore, it was necessary to search for another theory that accounted for the knife or blade. Robles provided the missing *theory or hypothesis* tonight, when he said that he had been *formulating or preparing* a study on the human sacrifices practiced by the Indians.[6] (Emphasis mine.)

Besides Chesterton, Bernal also exhibits a blend of Raymond Chandler and Ian Fleming. His pedestrian language can be attributed to the first. Bernal follows in the footsteps of the two masters by offering knowledge of the universe through an omnisicent narrator, grafted onto the mind of the detective (though at times he lends this voice to his prosaic García.) Like the Fleming of *Casino Royale,* for Bernal, sex and women play only supporting roles. As opposed to James Bond, Garcia does not know his enemies. And though in *The Big Sleep* he introduces us to an urban microcosm, both Bernal and Fleming heighten suspense through a series of crucially important diplomatic events.

It may be that Rafael Bernal is not a memorable writer; that being so, the obscurity into which he has plunged is not only inevitable but fitting. But there is room for suspicion that the severe judgment which he has avoided merits a refutation. María del Carmen Millán, who included him in her famous 1976 anthology of great Mexican storytellers,[7] apparently indulged just such a hunch. Taibo II is another writer who admires Bernal's pioneering work.

14

Carlos Fuentes

IF there is anyone in Latin America (and synedochically, in Mexico) who personifies the assimilation and adaptation of diverse "subgenres," who revalued literary currents and adapted them for his own use, it is Fuentes, born in 1928. From *Aura,* a collage paying tribute to Henry James and his *The Aspen Papers,* to Stevenson in *The Strange Case of Dr. Jekyll and Mr. Hyde;* and to Quevedo, the *conceptista* of "Alejado en la paz de estos desiertos . . . ,"[1] all the way to *Christopher Unborn,* an authentic recycling example, that brings Aldous Huxley, James Joyce, and George Orwell back to life, this writer is perhaps the most cosmopolitan figure in national letters, the most foreign Mexican of them all.

Dividing the history of Mexican letters into "before" and "after " Tlatelolco creates a difficulty when one attempts to study Fuentes' work. Despite the fact that his first collection of stories, *Los días enmascarados,* is from 1954, and his first novel, *Where the Air Is Clear,* came out four years later, one can detect a stylistic change beginning with *Aura* and *La muerte de Artemio Cruz* (The Death of Artemio Cruz, both from 1962), both of which are narrated in a second person like that of Michel Butor in *La modification* (1957). But it is after *Cambio de piel* (A Change of Skin, 1967) that the author ventured into modernist techniques approximating Joyce and the *nouveau roman,* which, in his earlier books, as previously mentioned, were more closely linked to Zola and Balzac. Since the seventies, Fuentes has been conversant with international literary currents, from which his work acquires influences and proposes both intersections and disparities—not only with his compatriots, but also with his contemporaries in Eastern Europe like Milan Kundera, in the United States like Philip Roth, or in South Africa like Nadine Gordimer. Therefore, Fuentes is a separate case, at odds with the closed, exclusive, and by some estimations parochial atmosphere of detective narrative art in Mexico.

The Hydra Head, his eighth novel, is without a doubt a homage to detective literature, an indirect tribute to *El complot mongol* (indirect indeed, because there is no evidence that Fuentes ever read Bernal).[2] It is a circular, enigmatic text which purports to uncover an international conspiracy but at the same time sets up a series of reflections which, like a maze of mirrors, reproduce images ad infinitum.[3] John Brushwood, in *La novela mexicana (1967–1982),* says that this book "confirms Fuentes' mastery as a narrator and newly evidences the fundamental importance of the fantastic in his novels, despite the fact that they address themes important to the modern age."[4]

In his Casanova-style adventures, the central character Félix Maldonado, alias Diego Velázquez, a man of humble origins, and son of a low-class petroleum worker, is simultaneously a detective and a Mexican bureaucrat (he is the head of the Department of Price Analysis in the Office of Industrial Development); as previously mentioned, though the two are linked, Maldonado is far from being Bernal's Filiberto García. He is a charismatic gigolo, flirtatious and suave, though possessed of an ambiguous identity—half Jewish, half Mexican.[5]

Though the majority of the action occurs in Mexico, there are scenes in the South of the United States. Signs of Fuentes' style and technique are present: an overdose of cultural references to the amorphousness of the Mexican personality. There is a foundation of Jewish-Mexican characters with loyalties to Israel or to the PLO. Maldonado works for an embryonic secret service, commanded by an anonymous, wealthy thirty-eight-year-old bachelor, a conservative nationalist with a grand mansion in Coyoacán. He had been one of Maldonado's colleagues at the National Autonomous University of Mexico and at Columbia in Manhattan.

The narrative voice is third person omniscient and, at first, objective. In the third section of the book, "War With The Hydra," we discover that the passages in the third person are part of a diary Maldonado has transported, transcribed by the secretary of his boss. The theme of the novel is the battle between Arabic, Israeli, and North American factions for the appropriation of Mexican oil, a plot which Fuentes dubs "Operation Guadalupe." Maldonado is contracted to defend the oil in 1973, at the apex of the political and financial crisis triggered by the Yom Kippur War in the Middle East. The passwords used by the secret service are quotations from Shakespeare. The detective is embroiled in dangerous, intrepid situations, and is even (falsely) accused of assassinating the president of the Republic. Fuentes infuses the text with religious symbols and technological mechanisms. Note the following passage, in which Maldonado's boss describes a secret, ancient chapel in his mansion, through which he guides his subordinate:

> The floor was paved with red volcanic rock; the wooden altar was painted white, with strips of gold molding. Above the reliquary and the tabernacle hung a painting of Our Lady of Guadalupe.
>
> I opened the tabernacle and removed the water-clear stone from Bermstein's ring. Holding it between thumb and index finger, I showed it to Felix. Inside this stone are two hundred images reduced to the size of pinpoints. Each one is printed on extremely thin film of high contrast and high photosensitive resolution. But these are not simply photographs that record the differing light intensities reflecting from the object, they're holograms that retain information about all phases of the light waves emanating from the object photographed.

He presses a button and a light shoots from the left eye of the Virgen de Guadalupe through the ring, which in turn projects virtual images revealing secrets about the conspiracy to take over Mexican petroleum. But the use of a religious fortress to conceal encoded information is a hallmark device of Fuentes, who is willing to depart from, without fully discarding, his at times irreverent, at times analytical attitude toward the archetypes of the national soul. From start to finish, Maldonado, in defending the petroleum, safeguards Mexican security while he investigates, like an intellectual James Bond, his own limits and weaknesses.

Fuentes, it remains to be said, is not a detective writer. *The Hydra Head* is only an experiment, albeit an exceedingly interesting one. As in the novels of Taibo II and Ramírez Heredia, and clearly, as in the author's previous books, Mexico City appears as one of the protagonists: the action begins in Sanborns restaurant on Madero avenue, in the center of the Capital; scenes are set in Los Pinos; in mass transit vehicles; in Polanco and the colony of Condesa, two Jewish communities; in the Zócalo and in Chapultepec. Unlike, for example, *An Easy Thing* by Taibo II, the slums are not present here. The political and aristocratic facets of Mexico attract Fuentes' attention, along with all of their biased transactions and hypocrisy.

There does not seem to be any connection between *The Hydra Head* and any of its detective predecessors in Mexico. In their place, there are ample references to Raymond Chandler, Dashiell Hammett, Lewis Carroll, and Edgar Allan Poe, as well as Shakespeare, in combination with a wide variety of *film noir*, which Fuentes notes and comments upon, making a passionate cinephile out of Maldonado. In the following passage, his wife foresees misfortune if he attends a party:

> Ruth had implored him, don't go to that party. Like Mary Astor in the final scene of *The Maltese Falcon*, incredulous, prepared to transform the lie of her love into the truth of her life if Humphrey Bogart would save her from the electric chair.[6]

Maldonado, I have said it before, is a Mexican James Bond, but with all the limitations of his native country: corruption, dishonesty, self-interest that tyrannizes over the collective. He moves through an atmosphere in which everything is burdened with bureaucracy and backhandedness is a way of life. He differs from Ian Fleming in several respects; first, because he is an intelligent individual but rarely firm about his decisions; he floats in an ether of ambiguous identity. Second, he cannot sleep with women without some type of commitment. Third, there are always identifying forces which inevitably cast him into an existential crisis. And finally, he defends Mexico from invasive powers while Bond travels through the world attacking communism and protecting the West.

15
Sergio Pitol, Rafael Ramírez Heredia, et al.

WE have already seen that the production of detective literature in Mexico is not limited to novels. Though in lesser quantity, stories and scripts produced for radio broadcasts do exist. There are also theatrical contributions, represented best by *El pequeño caso de Jorge Livído* by Sergio Magaña, which premiered in 1961 in a production by the actor and promoter Manolo Fábregas, and which opened again in 1978 at the Teatro de la Nacion directed by Rafael López Miarnau. The drama focuses on the loyalties of a policeman, who, as a participant in officialdom, must balance his individual interests with those of his fellow men.

There is also Emilio Carballido with *Relojero de Córdoba,* a work set in the Colony, about mythomaniac Martín Gama, who invents a never-committed crime and ends up in the dungeons of the Inquisition. Vicente Leñero joins Carballido with his *Nadie sabe nada* about the unsolved political assassination of journalist Manuel Buendía, columnist for *Excélsior;* the play was produced in the Teatro El Galeón and directed by Luis de Tavira (1988). Leñero indirectly accuses President Miguel de la Madrid of having ordered the crime. The play provoked tumult and controversy and the production company, the National Institute of Bellas Artes, closed it to the public, which caused a scandal that reached publications as distant as the *New York Times.*[1] Leñero also created the stage adaptation of *Los albañiles,* which will be discussed in part 3.

Other titles should appear alongside the aforementioned novels: Enrique F. Gual, in charge of introducing Sherlock Holmes in weekly installments in 1952–53 under the aegis of Editorial Albatros, published three narratives of his own: *El crimen de la obsidiana* (1942), *Asesinato en la plaza* (1946), and *El caso de los Leventheris* (1946); the Spaniard Max Aub, who lived in Mexico during his exile during the Civil War, wrote *Crímenes ejemplares* (1972) based on the crime pages of the yellow press;[2] José Zamora wrote *Desdémona en apuros* (1980) and *El collar de Jessica Rock-*

son (1980), whose detective, Vicente Camacho, is also called Sherlock Holmes or the "Mexican Maigret;" and also noteworthy are *Desnudarse o morir* (1957), by Miguel Ángel Mora; Luis Arturo Ramos, author of *Violeta-Perú* (1979); *Sobre esta piedra* (1981)[3] by Carlos Eduardo Turrón; and *Pretexta* (1979) by Federico Campbell.

Among all of such novels, perhaps the most noteworthy is *El desfile del amor* by Sergio Pitol (born in 1933), based on a celebrated comedy by Lubitsch. The novel won the Herralde Prize in Spain and was published in 1984. It takes place in 1942 in Mexico City, though all is seen in retrospect through the eyes of a historian, Miguel del Solar, a resident of England who returns to Mexico— a building on Minerva St., to be exact—to investigate the details of a murder that had occurred when he was only ten. The victim is Erich, the son of a German married to one of Solar's relatives.

Pitol uses the incident as a springboard to paint a portrait of Mexican society during World War II, including the pressure oil corporations exerted upon Mexico when the country declared war against Germany and immigrants began to pour into Mexico City— wealthy Jewish businessmen, Trotsky and his disciples, Soviet secret service agents, North Americans and Germans, Spanish Republicans, and so on. Therefore, the detective act generates a mosaic of xenophobic, religious, economic and sociocultural attitudes, which together form the text's genuine focus. The manner in which the historian examines the details of the incident, interviews actors and witnesses, and studies the local and international press suggests to the reader that Mexican reality is reluctant to be disclosed, that confusion reigns and truth never emerges with ease.

Another author of importance who has contributed to the genre is Rafael Ramírez Heredia. Born in 1942, Heredia is a journalist, essayist, and short-story writer. In 1984 he won the Juan Rulfo International Prize for the Short Story, awarded in Paris, for his collection *El Rayo Macoy*. His themes are always uniquely Mexican. They generally draw from national folklore and invoke the slang of the capital city or of distinct provinces. *La jaula de Dios,* (1989)[4] an echo of *Where the Air Is Clear,* is another crucible which examines the vicissitudes of Mexico City in its multiple manifestations, ranging from the love affairs of high-school students, rape of minors, crimes of thugs, blind players who stage circuses at banquets, to the social climbing of public dignitaries, a blind bolero singer, and so on. Like Aub, he continually supplements his narrative with facts extracted from the crime pages and with commentaries of editorialists in publications like *Excélsior, Siempre!* and *Unomásuno.*

Heredia, who lived for a time in Spain, authored two novels which belong to the genre: *Trampa de metal* (1979)[5] and *Muerte en la carretera* (1986).[6] Unlike those of his compatriots (excepting Taibo II), these novels abound with violent scenes and do not exclude alcohol and sex. They bear little resemblance to the classical, traditional model, in which characters solve mysteries; Heredia writes hard-boiled detective novels.

His protagonist is Ifigenio Clausel, "among friends, If," a detective from Coyoacán, a man in his forties who drives a tiny old Renault, clashes with bodyguards, and penetrates into the hidden depths of politics and prostitution in Mexico.

In the beginning of *Muerte en la carretera* If is summoned to the Chamber of Deputies in the center of the capital by his friend Justino Cabrera, a deputy, who wishes to use his services. Silvino Arruza, a federal deputy for the 21st Electoral District, had been murdered on the road to Tampico. His car had been sprayed with bullets during an ambush. After his fees are paid, If embarks upon a complicated investigation which takes him from Tampico all the way to Chiapas—that is to say, he traverses the Republic from one end to the other. On the way, he crosses paths with knaves, thugs, drunks, and corrupt diplomats.

The narrative is always in the third person, except when If reflects upon his actions, at which time he assumes a first-person introspective voice. I have reproduced here one passage from the opening, after If, in Tampico, receives a telephone tip-off that enemies are already pursuing him:

> I can't even say I know anything concrete. Nothing concrete, it was only something about where they were going to catch me. So already they're hot on my heels. That call wasn't coincidental, someone knows that I'm here, on this shore. I'm being made a fool of, no more bowing like a little Chinaman and going from one place to another like a beggar. *Ay,* Ifigenio, if you would just leave all of this foolishness behind—but no, no more are you going to run away as soon as you see something upsetting, run away and let it be, never stopping to think about where the next step will take you. But this Deputy thing isn't the same as looking for fleas in a dungheap, no, here everything is very fucked up and if you try to be too clever you're going to put yourself smack in the middle of it all.[7]

His admiration of Philip Marlowe is clear in the language, the passages of stream of consciousness, and the harsh rhythm of the action. Once in awhile, *Muerte en la carretera* makes a reference to other novels of the genre: If, for example, reads *El complot mongol* at the beginning. When the enemies hold him captive, they threaten him by reminding him that both Bernal and Carlos Fuentes from *The Hydra Head* believe that the easiest way of untangling webs of facts and puzzles is to kill the detective himself. If, of course, is terrified.

The ultimate outcome, as one might expect, ends rather more simply. Silvino Arruza has a chance at the governorship of Jalapa, Veracruz. But he has competitors, among them another deputy, Luciano Ordaz. When a dear friend of Ordaz's performs a striptease at a party, Arruza or one of his lackeys snapped photographs, planning to distribute them to the mass media. Ordaz, his character defamed, had no other choice but murder.

Up to this point, none of the aforementioned titles nor detectives have attained the popularity of the sagas featuring Héctor Belascoarán Shayne, without a doubt the most dashing and enduring of Mexican private eyes.

16

Paco Ignacio Taibo II

Sherlock Holmes is possibly the only character in fiction who has become a permanent fixture. That is to say, he is a human being with a "real" life (the word, however, infuriates Holmes faithfuls), who lives in London and lived at precisely 221-B Baker St. Indeed, there is another character who has passed from fiction into life: Don Quixote, and, attached to him, his constant companion Sancho. It is not mere chance that Holmes and Watson are similar to the Castilian pair two centuries their senior. Holmes, tall and thin, attacks criminal giants and converts them into windmills, or perhaps pinwheels, while Watson, short and stout, recommends prudence as if he were a safety inspector. Holmes, addicted to drugs and music. Quixote, addicted to books, and another drug which he drinks undiluted. Watson, a realist, given to predicting one or two actual disasters. Sancho, a man of restraint who demonstrates the caution of the Castille.

    —*Holmes, Sweet Holmes,* Guillermo Cabrera Infante

THE Cuban novelist presented this analogy in an article on the centenary of the celebrated protagonist created by Arthur Conan Doyle.[1] There is, of course, another detective who, like Holmes, maintains an address: Héctor Belascoarán Shane. He lives on a street in the central zone of Mexico City called Article 123. He shares his room and office with Gilberto the plumber, Carlos Vargas the upholsterer, and Gallo Villarreal, expert in deep drainage. In addition, like Don Quixote, he attempts—sometimes against his will—to combat and exorcise the ghosts of the collective soul.

Belascoarán Shayne appears in more than six novels and is inspired by Philip Marlowe, Chandler's creation. His journeys take him to several regions of the Mexican republic, from Oaxaca to Guerrero, but he is a bohemian who frequents the bars of the municipality of Azcapotzalco.

The detective has the same physical appearance as his creator,

Paco Ignacio Taibo II. He is short, smokes heavily, and enjoys watching the smoke drift from his cigarette. He is constantly alone, works at night, sleeps during the day, and usually places black patches over his eyelids in order to sleep. His favorite drink is the *cuba libre*. At first glance he seems rude and uncouth but in reality he is good-natured. Like Marlowe, he has a love-hate relationship with Mexico City, *his* city, which he views as a giant garbage receptacle. He is the type of man who constantly complains about police and governmental corruption, but will not think twice about offering a bribe of as much as fifteen hundred dollars to obtain valuable information.

A commentary about the name is due. Belascoarán, the last name, is Basque in origin; Shayne, on the other hand, makes him a distant relative Michael Shayne, the Miami detective created by Brett Holliday (pseudonym of Davis Dresser) who is a football fanatic, drinks Martell, and is based on a Mexican whom Holliday met while working on a petroleum tankard after finishing school. Like Marlowe, our acclimatized Mexican hero possessed a university education, a beautiful house, a spouse, and a salary of 22,000 *pesos* a month as an engineer. But he sacrificed everything to be his own boss. Because his income is irregular, he manages to pay for his tortillas by entering a television contest—or, he simply waits for a case.

High-ranking politicians, millionaires, young women, and old friends seek his expertise. His investigations have a national character. He is frightened and his life has been threatened. In the end, it was he and no one else who solved the case of the mysterious death of the porter for a First Division team from Jalisco, and investigated the frauds in the construction of the Basílica de Guadalupe. Moreover, in *An Easy Thing*,[2] perhaps his most widely read novel, he briefly introduced the notion that Emiliano Zapata, the legendary hero of the Mexican Revolution assumed to have been assassinated on a Chinameca ranch in 1919, had never perished but was sequestered in a cave in the state of Morelos, out of which he directed guerrilla activity in El Salvador, Nicaragua, and South America.

What differentiates him from the rest of the Mexican detectives, including Péter Pérez de Peralvillo and Ramírez Heredia's If, is Shayne's passion for deciphering national history. He is always restless and eager to examine macho psychology, the popularity of boxing and bullfighting, drugs and politics, and he offers an answer to the question, "Why is the Mexican soul so confused, so suffocated by an inferiority complex, deficient confidence, introversion and dishonesty?"

Paco Ignacio Taibo II, the executive vice-president of the International Association of Crime Writers, was born in Spain in 1949 and moved to Mexico in 1958, where he settled permanently; he was naturalized in 1980. His training is not in literature but in history: He graduated from the National Autonomous University of Mexico and until only recently had a professorship at the National Metropolitan-Unity University of Azcapotzalco. He has dabbled in journalism. He has published history books and narratives, and editions of representative works on national political events. He professes a leftist, Marxist ideology; thus the epigraphs interspersed throughout his work—each chapter invariably begins with one—come from Engels, Proudhon, but also from Hegel, Nietzsche, great jazz musicians, Cuban ballads, Roberto Fernández Retamar, Bertolt Brecht, or Heinrich Böll.

Taibo II is the son of Paco Ignacio Taibo, movie critic and novelist, author of *Siempre Dolores* and *De algún tiempo a esta parte.*[3] Among his books one finds a chronicle of Ernesto "Ché" Guevara in the battle of Santa Clara, the 1958 masterstroke that toppled the dictatorship of Fulgencio Batista in Cuba.[4] He edited and introduced *Bajando la frontera,* a 1985 collection of texts by North American journalists like John Reed, John Kenneth Turner, Richard Francis Phillips, and Mike Gold, all communists who, during the Revolution of 1910, served as reporters from South of the Río Grande for United States dailies. The majority of these articles had never been translated to the Spanish and together provide a disquieting showcase of human anxieties and the heterogenous politics of the so-called "Colossus of the North."[5] Another valuable book by Taibo II is *El liberalismo mexicano,* a detailed study of the origins of syndicalism in Mexico, the nineteenth-century strikes and struggles for legitimacy. José C. Valadés, the original author, had written the text but had poor luck publishing it during his lifetime; at the beginning of this century, many renowned historians had acquired copies of the manuscript and had plagiarized it. Taibo II reconstructed the text, some parts of which had been extracted, and, having received it from the hands of Valadés's son, he annotated and published it, elevating the work and its author to its deserved place.[6]

Taibo II's detective repertoire includes *Días de combate* (1976), *An Easy Thing* (1977); *No habrá final feliz* (No Happy Ending, 1981); *Algunas nubes* (Some Clouds, 1985); *Sombra de la sombra* (The Shadow of the Shadow, 1986); *La vida misma* (Life Itself), which won the prize for the best detective novel from the International Association of Detective Writers (AIEP) in 1987; and *Regreso a la misma ciudad y bajo la lluvia* (1989).[7] Not all feature Belascoarán Shayne as the central sleuth. *The Shadow of the Shadow,* for example, is a historical novel set in 1922, which has both a poet and a professional journalist, respectively, in the duo of Fermín Valencia and Pioquinto Manterola. These characters attempt to unravel the mysterious death of a musician in the public plaza. In the process of collecting clues involving the incident, they unleash a flood of political intrigues: They discover a secret plot engineered by U.S. petroleum corporations, which conspire to foment a counterrevolution in certain territories of the Mexican geography and to provoke a secession that would convert the lands into North American property. Obviously, judging from the political and financial implications of the matter, the adventure only could have occurred before the regime of Lázaro Cárdenas and the nationalization of petroleum.

But Belascoarán Shayne is the most celebrated character created by Taibo II. He speaks a vulgar language, replete with malapropisms, offensive insults, and street syntax. It is similar to the Julio Cortázar's verbal games, which Shayne periodically mentions and emulates. He is an alcoholic, a recluse, hypocritical on the outside and sincere on the inside, a humanitarian individual who catapults himself into terrible predicaments. He is a man emotionally moved by social inequality, by the chaos represented by Mexico City, by injustice. The following extract comes from *Regreso a la misma ciudad y bajo la lluvia,* in which Belascoarán Shayne loses the vision in one eye in December:

> He passed among the small shops on Insurgentes, crossed the Metro square at a tired trot, went into Chapultepec Avenue, considering— with his healthy eye—the offerings of the city. Misery attacked with all the fury of the pre-Christmas season. Underemployment was overwhelming. A wave of Mexicans who were searching for a *peso* with sad and feverish eyes came at him from all sides. The hands of beggars were more cracked and unsteady than usual. How could there be solidarity with all of this?, Héctor asked himself. How can one coexist with this without rotting away with sadness?, he moaned. Once, Elisa had read out loud from a Cortázar text about the train station in New Delhi and the uneasiness that had seized her while reading it, how you can't live alongside the dark places of this world without becoming a little cynical, a lot son of a bitch. Cortázar was right. He said it in the language of the fifties, that there was no peaceful coexistence between the parts of society that kept falling into pieces, with the other part,

your part, that kept falling down. "For a Cyclops it might be easier, you only have to close one eye," he said, but even he didn't dare smile at the joke.[8]

Raymond Chandler, in "Casual Notes on the Mystery Novel,"[9] says that the only way to mock readers is to force them to apply their logic to the wrong problems. This is precisely what Taibo II does: His novels focus more on history and urban violence (it revolves around the capital as if it were the axis of the globe), and less on logic. In *An Easy Thing*, for example, three adventures occur simultaneously, but in the end their paths do not converge. The prose is riddled with vague, scattered facts, none of which contribute to the development of the plot. The purpose of the narrative, however, is clear: in a modernist flight of fancy, the author attempts to creative a narrative mimetic of the dynamics of chaos. His fantasy is always fragmentary, incomplete. Just when we think we are getting somewhere, a vexing turn will reveal further angles on a subject. And the descriptions are always Hemingwayesque—we receive only what Belascoarán Shayne sees and thinks, with no elaboration and always in an economical, rigorous manner.

It is important to see Taibo II as a direct product of the generation of "la Onda" and the phenomenon of Tlatelolco—as a follower, in some ways, of Gustavo Sáinz and José Agustín, whose politics were decidedly antiestablishment. One can detect all of this in the attitude of Belascoarán Shayne, who never looks askance at a member of his social sphere, and yet is a rebel who doubts the honesty of anyone who stands in his way. Taibo II's membership to this generation attracts him to the detective novel, and also transforms him into an unconventional academic.

Evidence of his heterogeneous, rebellious style is *Arcángeles: Cuatro historias poco ortodoxas de revolucionarios,* a collection of profiles of marginal European and Mexican revolutionaries. It was published for the first time in literary supplements like *Unomásuno* and *Siempre!.* One describes the life and death of Max Holz, a syndicalistic German activist who was murdered by the Soviets in 1933. Another text analyzes the adventures of an eventual follower of Ricardo Flores Magón, the politician and writer who instigated the socialist Revolution of 1910. A third work speaks of the attempts of Diego Rivera, David Alfaro Siqueiros, and José Clemente Orozco to form an artist's union in 1922. All are experiments in historical narrative. Using curious historical events as a base, Taibo II injects passion, objectivity, and suspense, and spins a literary web that is both enjoyable and informative.[10]

There is a symmetry between Taibo II and Manuel Vázquez Montalbán, the Spanish novelist, essayist, and creator of the detective Pepe Carvalho in novels like *Yo maté a Kennedy* (1972) and *Tatuaje* (1974). In addition to their friendship, both writers share an ideology of the left (obvious in the scenes of the Central Committee and the Communist Party). Exercising this ideology in the detective novel, curiously enough, serves to criticize and therefore protest political and social degeneration. The sequence of events is rapid, progressive; their novels never indulge in superfluous or redundant descriptions; their private eyes are merciless and vulgar; the narrative language is violent. Although they declare a passion for politics, they never proselytize, and nor do they embrace demagoguery. Due to this Marxist perspective of literature and the world, the two have achieved enormous popularity in their respective countries.

Another parallel can be drawn between Taibo II and Dorothy L. Sayers, deceased in 1957, the British detective writer who was a medieval essayist who prepared an annotated edition of Dante Alighieri's *Divine Comedy*. Her detective, Lord Peter Wimsey, ironic and sophisticated, might be viewed as the antithesis of Belasocarán Shayne. Even so, the two authors share an attraction to both academics and detective literature, and their investigators are symbols of their respective national idiosyncracies.

Like the greater portion of detective literature in Mexico, the books of Taibo II have suffered a dearth of review and criticism. However, the moment they appear on the bookshelves they become bestsellers and immediately go into reprint. Several resemblances can be located between Taibo II and Raymond Chandler, among them the fact that both have created modern gentlemen in search of hidden truths—in the case of the Mexican, historical truths. Their private eyes are common men of the modern age, however unusual they might be, who take justice into their own hands. Moreover, the two authors are not interested in imposing order upon their cases, a task they leave to Lord Wimsey, Hercule Poirot, or Armando Zozaya; what they desire is knowledge of crucial social secrets. Both mantain an ambiguous relationship with their cities, Mexico City and Los Angeles. The following quote comes from *No Happy Ending*: "Take yourself lightly, but take the city seriously, the city, that inscrutable porcupine bristling with quills and soft wrinkles. Shit, he was in love with Mexico City. Another possible love on his list. A city to love with abandon.

Passionately, mildly."[11] But perhaps most important is the language of these books: morbid, immoral, and violent universe manifests itself in their vocabulary of choice. In other words, the vulgar, unrefined, and ungrammatical idiom becomes the essential force driving home the images.

It is necessary to present one more comparison, one which returns to the argument in the epigraph by Cabrera Infante. According to John Dickson Carr, Arthur Conan Doyle, with his cult of the intellect and his self-sufficient hero, wrote the Sherlock Holmes series to defray living expenses (as a doctor of minimal prestige, his career had not proved satisfactorily lucrative).[12] But bored with the adventures of his protagonist, in *The Memoirs of Sherlock Holmes* (1894), he attempted to do away with the main character. The uproar from fans was such that the writer was obliged to resuscitate him and print several more volumes. Taibo II, in a tribute to Holmes, describes the death of Belascoarán Shayne in the ultimate chapter of *No Happy Ending*—by which time, the detective had already appeared in five novels as well as several short stories. "It was raining hard when he got off the buss on Articulo 123," Taibo II writes. Belascoarán Shayne, walking around neighborhood, was hiding everywhere he could from the terrible downpour. He stopped to buy a bag of donuts and three cups of coffee for his partners when a suspicious automobile approached him. The first shot missed him by three feet and ended up hitting a shoeshine boy inside a Chinese restaurant.

> Héctor threw the coffee and donuts to the ground, grabbed his gun, and ran diagonally across the half-flooded street.
>
> He fired as he ran. His second shot hit one of the Halcones trying to get out of the car without sticking his feet in a sewer grate. His next shot hit another one in the leg. He'd almost reached the cover of the newspaper kiosk on the corner when a shotgun blast caught him mid-torso and lifted his torn, broken body into the air.
>
> He fell facedown in a puddle, near death. His hand groped in the dirty water, trying to grab on to something, trying to stop something, trying to keep something from slipping away. Then he lay motionless. A man approached and kicked him twice in the face. They got back into their cars and drove off.
>
> The rain continued to fall on the shattered body of Héctor Belascoarán Shayne.[13]

As in the case of Conan Doyle, the fanaticism of his followers refused to allow the hero to stay dead. Taibo II, in the "Author's Note" of *Regreso a la misma ciudad y bajo la lluvia*, the subsequent novel, plays with the idea of resurrection in the popular Mexican context:

> Do not ask me how and when Héctor Belascoarán Shayne will reappear. I have no answer . . . The magic is not totally up to me. Appeal to the cultural traditions of a country whose history abounds with returns. The Vampire returned, the Saint returned (in cinematographic form), even Demetrio Vallejo returned after his prison sentence, Benito Juárez returned from the Paso del Norte . . . This particular revival began two years ago in the city of Zacatecas, when a public conference demanded that Belascoarán come back to life by an almost unanimous vote (short by only one). This happened several more times before various audiences, in different cities, and the polls were accompanied by a lengthy series of letters. It seems that, according to the sentiment of the readers, our character has not yet met his end. Even this author believes that a few more stories remain to be told in the Belascoarán saga.[14]

Perhaps this is the most effective device by which to measure the reception and interest in this type of popular literature and, in particular, in this author. As Bermúdez has said, Taibo II is attracted by violence and the image of the detective as a superhero of the underdeveloped. In the interview with Torres, she says, "Action and adventure matter to him, but not the logical puzzling, not the game of chess, to put it one way, that opens up between the writer and the reader, which in reality is quite challenging."[15]

Héctor Belascoarán Shayne, then, is the natural incarnation of the Mexican detective. Alongside Ramírez Heredia and the three authors examined in part 3, his cases, investigating the deaths of magicians, soccer players, corrupt politicians, and gangsters, always against a backdrop of a chaotic, decadent city teeming with mystery, rivalry, and poverty, have inspired an expansion. More than anything else, this climax phase of Mexican police and detective letters begins in the seventies.

Part 3

17

Revolutionizing the Formula

WHAT characteristics do the works of Helú, Bernal, Sergio Pitol, Solana, Usigli, Carlos Fuentes, and the rest share? Is it possible to talk about a connected, coordinated movement with one unique vision of the world? The answer to the second question is no. With very few exceptions—among them *Muerte en la carretera* and Bermúdez's commentaries—it is difficult to prove that these texts have any awareness, albeit minimal, of their precursors. From *Ensayo de un crimen* onward, nearly all of these novels are written as if in a vacuum, always emulating exterior models, ignorant of the domestic scene. By extension, one could claim that Mexican detective writers, although cohabiting the same city and belonging to the same culture, are further from their colleagues than from the late Hammett, Poe, or MacDonald.

The denouement of the same problems and a common native idiosyncracy unite them. From Péter Pérez to Héctor Belascoarán and If, the police are regarded with distrust, like a focus of unhealthy morality. Order, in their eyes, is a contrivance in an environment where disorder is natural.

Ramírez Heredia, Pitol, and Taibo II pay tribute to the Distrito Federal, with its mysterious niches, its labyrinthine passions, and its growing misery. They describe markets, factories, bars, slums, violent areas, prostitutes on corners, sewers, government offices. Pitol and Taibo II especially applaud the juxtaposition of past and present, yesterday and today. They show, through the mingling of ages and areas in the city's architecture and in various metropolitan attitudes, how deeply the country has suffered, trying to adapt to modern technology and rhythm.

Two of the most attractive themes are oil and religion. Fuentes and Taibo II make the black gold a wellspring of national pride and independence. Both, just like Bernal, examine sacramental symbols as targets of popular devotion, in an attempt to demonstrate how embedded faith is in Mexico. Another theme that frequently appears is the pre-Columbian past (Aztec, Mayan, and so on) and the revolutionary past (Emiliano Zapata, Pancho Villa, Francisco I. Madero), which makes this literary subgenre into a type of laboratory where they can test collective identity and the condition of the nation.

Up until this point only the more or less experimental detective contribution has been studied. These authors not only respect the elements of the generic formula, at least to some extent, but, in its practice, they emulate and pay an implicit tribute to the foreign model. Thus theirs can be seen as a labor of "stylization," to use Bakhtin's terminology. That which is Mexican in these novels lies in the language, the criticism of the corrupt order and the State, or the peculiar "Mexican" metabolism of their detectives and secret agents.

It is curious to note how, before Tlatelolco, the magnet that drew the detective novelists was the British model, with its "classic," traditional formula. After the student massacre in 1968, the most rude, hard-boiled, and least complacent element of the North American style captured the artistic favor. Why? Because on one hand it promotes the vociferous denouncement of the fraud of the political regimen, without caution or fear. On the other, in a society controlled by violence, it portrays the detective as a kind of "evil," not an intellectual.

These experiments have allowed introspection into the collective past and personality. They investigate, in the psychological tradition of Octavio Paz and Samuel Ramos, the complexes, deformations, the spiritual battle waged within the Mexican spirit. For Pitol, literature is an exercise in meticulous style while for Taibo II it is a vehicle through which alternate worlds are invented, never far removed from reality. With an uninhibited bearing, Taibo II packs his paragraphs with vituperations and vulgarities, malapropisms and linguistic deformations, the same heard everyday on the street. The clash with authority and power is carried out at many levels: grammatical, in the actions of Héctor Belascoarán Shayne, and in the description of his environment. Chaos, for Ramírez Heredia and Taibo II, is order. It is not their duty to remedy it, only to study it through parody.

Furthermore, although there were a few examples of stories and theater, it is interesting that in Mexico, unlike Buenos Aires, the detective genre medium par excellence, the writers' favorite, is the novel. Why? Because in it one can speculate, prowl, and even tease, pleasures that impassion the Mexican and cannot be achieved in a story. Furthermore, theater can be "too" public, and there are things that cannot be said aloud.

A misinformed reader might think, at this point, that detective literature's contribution in Mexico has been a conservative force, rebellious only in that it negates some formulaic precepts, like making the detective into Robin Hood or not obliging Good to prevail over Evil. One might think that imitation has not effected a revolutionizing, drastic change, an incisive transformation of the foreign model, grafted to the national corpus of literature. This reader would be wrong.

Three authors are reserved for this chapter: Vicente Leñero, Jorge Ibargüengoitia, and José Emilio Pacheco. It is true that all three began their careers before the massacre at Tlatelolco. Nonetheless, their work is marked by modernist, ludic, and irreverent tendencies because 1968 scarred them at a political level, and at an artistic level invited them to take more liberties, to revolutionize. Their detective work is fascinating because their affiliation with the genre is transient, implying that none considers himself a detective novelist, but rather each borrowed only certain elements from the formula, not just recirculate them with another facade, but to "reformulate" them.

The decision to group them together is based on the narrative disposition that they show in their works, which can be categorized as what Bakhtin labels "parodical stylization"; that is, when the imitation of a literary genre involves renovation and even transformation, in such a way that while they do not exceed the boundaries of the genre, the narrations acquire a life of their own. The three have given light to "innovating texts," not uniquely at a linguistic level but also structurally and technically.

As children of Tlatelolco, they were not afraid to expose the gory details beneath the country's superficial existence. But much more than for Taibo II or Ramírez Heredia, their apprenticeship also came under James Joyce, the French *nouveau roman*, Nabokov, Kafka, and Borges. This bestows a more serious pretension on their literary texts. They are less fleeting and forgettable, but without any contempt for the thriller, which they recognize as their own literary impetus and an honest product of popular culture. Their books, therefore, compared with their predecessors', are more sophisticated; their style is more ambitious, careful, meticulous, and limpid.

Before embarking into this section it is worthwhile to consider the view proposed by Dennis Porter, the previously mentioned North American critic, author of *The Pursuit of Crime,* regarding

Borges's detective contribution. He coins the phrase "anti-detection" and uses it to address the authors who "flip" the formula for detective fiction. Porter selects Nabokov, Henry James, and Kafka to illustrate this maneuver, and one could also add Friedrich Dürrenmatt to the same list. In these modernists' (in the Anglo-Saxon sense, rather than the Hispanic) texts, the detective's deduction does not belie man's supreme intellect, order, or morality, but a new and strange code of uncertainties. The reader ends their works invariably disillusioned: when it seems that the plot's central enigma has been resolved, it turns out we are mired in obfuscation of greater dimensions; upon carefully following the steps of the formula, the private eye (and the readers along with him) soon falls upon a suicidal vacuum.

Porter especially cites "La muerte y la brújula" (Death and the Compass), Borges's story which appeared in Buenos Aires, in *Ficciones* in 1944: Erik Lönnrot, the detective, battles his archenemy, Red Scharlach, who leaves clues through which the investigator deduces he will soon commit a fourth and final murder, in a specific site in the city, at a given date and time. But upon arriving at the scene of the crime, to his surprise, Lönnrot discovers that he himself is to be the victim, and is killed. Porter comments: "The intricate web in which Borges's anti-Dupin is trapped reveals its diabolic rationality. More often than not, however, the experience of Borges's narrators and scholar/heroes is of a universe which abounds in pointless symmetries and in maniacal repetitions'. If they find a path through the labyrinth, it is only to discover that the exit is really an entrance, that the labyrinth solved is no more than a labyrinth within a greater labyrinth. Problem solving is shown to occur, as on a chessboard, only within predetermined and therefore artificial limits. In Borges's fictional universe a checkmate achieved in accordance with the traditional rules of the game turns out to be a suicidal move on a suddenly expanded board."[1]

Porter similarly analyzes *The Turn of the Screw* and *The Process*. He concludes that while the traditional detective formula is repeated to the point of exhaustion in the contemporary thriller, it has been the work of the post-World War II modernists to utilize the same elements to ridicule the arrogant western intellect and Occamistic and Cartesian logic. This implies that authors like Nabokov or Borges have shifted the genre from the popular sphere to the elitist, and that postwar narrative art feeds on certain "sub-genres," revitalizing them.

The aspiration of part 3 is to demonstrate how "anti-deduction" acquires another character, wider and more multifaceted, in Mexico: the detective in *Morirás lejos* is only the reader; our rationality doubts itself because there are no final and incontrovertible conclusions in Pacheco's text. Similarly, Leñero uses the formula in *Los albañiles* only to play with suspense, because at the end he does not offer any solution to the case of the murdered watchman. In *The Dead Girls*, Ibargüengoitia, for his part, reproduces the pursuit of clues and trails surrounding Las Poquianchis, a group of prostitutes subdued and riddled with bullets by their matrons, offering not just a thriller, but a majestic showcase of Mexican behaviors and abuses. As will be seen, the three utilize the detective formula as a trampoline to elaborate a social chronicle, a political satire, or an enigmatic mosaic of possibilities without any solution.

Aimed at a more refined readership, these authors' works distance themselves from the strictly popular scene, bringing the detective novel to a more aesthetically educated reader. Thus it is necessary to reconceptualize "anti-deduction." It will not only be understood as a mechanism to challenge the arrogant western intellect, but will also serve to demonstrate that the genre's construction can be dismantled, its fabric unwoven.

18
Vicente Leñero

Born in Guadalajara in 1933, Vicente Leñero has been a journalist, novelist, and playwright, as well as a founding member and collaborator of *Proceso*. From his pen have come *Los periodistas* (1978), which recounts the 1974 scandal in which president Luis Echeverría took military measures against the harsh criticism of Julio Scherer García, the director of the newspaper *Excélsior,* occupying the paper's offices and dismissing the staff, *El evangelio de Lucas Gavilán* (1979); *Redil de ovejas* (1973); *Estudio Q* (1965); and *El garabato* (1967). The last two play with the elements that arose from metafiction, and both have murders or detective plots. Although their affiliation to Helú's notion of chronology is weak, it should still be considered.

Estudio Q is constructed as a *telenovela,* or soap opera, based on the biography of Alejandro Jiménez Brunetière, a famous *telenovela* star. As the plot progresses, Alex's scenes and his discussions with the stage director and with the screenwriter, Gladys Monroy, end up as part of the same *telenovela*. In other words, like in Shakespeare's *Hamlet* when the prince performs a play for his stepfather and mother, Leñero introduces one reality within another. The necessary elements subsequently appear leading the reader to believe that, at long last, what he or she is reading is unquestionably reality. But once more it is a lie; Alex, his love, and his fury end up being the biography of Brunetière. Marcela Fernández Violante made a movie based on *Estudio Q* (1981), starring Juan Ferrara and Helena Rojo. The progression of the plot was based on the unfolding of scenes, like a game of mirrors wherein the line between reality and fiction is blurred.

In both novel and film there is a death: Alex, supposedly, will commit suicide in front of the cameras, as the only way to disrupt the cycle of turmoil, to destroy the web of metafictions that confuse and imprison him. "He fell suddenly to the shock of his colleagues and staff, incredulous at what they saw," assures Leñero, "but immediately convinced that it would be useless to try to return the life that he himself had taken away."[1] Is he really dead? While doubt does reign, the adherence to the thriller tradition is debatable.

When all is said and done, Alex's public death, forced by his two colleagues' tricks, the abundance of witnesses, clues, and so on, and the invitation the author extends to the reader to determine what is certain and what is not, granting him the role of the distant, passive investigator (the opposite, as will be seen, of Pacheco's maneuver in *Morirás lejos*), all this, although there is no detective per se, demonstrates suspense and the use of certain elements of the formula. But once again the trickery becomes clear, and ultimately Leñero seems to be more interested in confusing reality and fantasy, and refuses to allow a logical explanation of the events.[2]

The same metafictitious embroglio appears in the structure of *El garabato*, one novel within another, about a third. It begins with a headline announcing *El garabato* de Vicente Leñero, followed by a two-page letter by Pablo Mejía H. thanking the author for so quickly locating an editor for his novel, *El garabato*, and discussing some of his Borgesian twists. Pablo Mejía H.'s *El garabato* continues, narrated by Fernando J. Moreno, a famous critic who has writer's block, preventing him from writing the "Great Mexican Novel." Moreno discusses his illicit love with Lucy and his incomplete reading of Fabián Mendizábal's *El garabato*. And the detective ingredient? Mendizábal's text discusses Rodolfo, a young Mexican, studying law, who accidentally becomes involved in a mystery-adventure which endangers his life. Rendezvous, critical commentaries on other commentaries, and reflections of reflections abound. As expected, nothing is resolved at the end, Rodolfo's adventures remain unconcluded, and the only achievement is to put doubt in the existence of Vicente Leñero himself, which means proceeding one step beyond *Estudio Q*.[3]

These two books illustrate Leñero's affection toward thrillers. There are two more, however, that present an unquestionable affiliation to the genre: the extraordinary *Los albañiles* (1964), winner of the Seix-Barral's Premio Biblioteca Breve[4]; and *Asesinato. El doble crimen de los Flores Muñoz* (1985).[5]

The first, a "parodical stylization" where a detective and a murder function as a pretext to elaborate an idiosyncratic examination of Mexican society, is perhaps the author's most celebrated work. It begins when don Jesús, an old watchman, perverse and corrupt, is found dead at a construction site in Mexico City. The passive voice of Detective Munguía—who is referred to as "the man with

the striped tie" throughout the book—is responsible for inter-
viewing all of the workers to find out who is to blame. There are
six suspects: Federico Zamora, the construction supervisor and
the boss's son; Jacinto and Patotas, two workers; a fifteen-year-
old laborer named Isidro; the plumber, Sergio Garcia; and Alvarez,
the maestro.

Leñero recreates each's argument in narrative, according to the
situation and the facts surrounding the crime. But instead of dismissing each possibility one by one, the six retain irrefutable logic
and coherence until the end. The final paragraph of the book is
surprising:

> (Munguía) walked all night and at six in the morning came to the corner
> of Cuauhtémoc and Concepción Béistigui. For a long while he contem-
> plated the building from the sidewalk in front. He crossed the street.
> He pushed on the iron door: through it, no more than five steps away,
> was a man wrapped to his head in a serape. He rubbed his hands over
> the embers where a small mug of coffee was heating up. The noise of
> the door made him straighten his head. The serape slipped down his
> back and fell to the ground.
> "Looking for someone?"
> Munguía took three steps forward. The man stood up.
> "Looking for someone?"
> "Are you the watchman?"
> "Yeah," the man said. "What can I do for you?"
> Munguía eyed him from head to toe.
> "Nothing," he took one more step. He smiled. "Nothing . . ."
> And he put a hand on his shoulder.[6]

The detective, without a solution, returns to the scene of the
crime, and discovers that the watchman is once again at his post.
Through eternal return, a symbolic cycle is constructed where
circumstances are repeated; because nothing changes and everything remains constant in the urban construction environment.[7]

The intrinsic value of the text lies in its form as much as its
content. It is composed of sequential monologues; in the majority
of cases, especially for the police interrogators, one can only know
who is talking by their grammatical rhythms (thus a polyphonic or
dialogic voice is created, as Bakhtin would say), because we lack
a direct identification. As Amelia S. Simpson affirms in her previously mentioned study of Latin American detective literature:

> Against the reductivism of the classic detective model with its comfort-
> ing allegory of justice and order, the elimination of the solution pro-

duces an expansive delineation of issues raised by the investigation of crime. Leñero careful constructs his novel to invite comparison with the conventional *novela de enigma,* that is, to assert the palimpsest nature of the text. By suppressing the solution, multiplying rather than eliminating suspects, and adopting a narrative technique that presents those suspects as disembodied, representative voices, he diverts the aim of the underlying, classic model from the identification of a culprit to the investigation of society.[8]

Luisa Josefina Ludmer has the same thesis; the novel as a whole, according to her, is a metaphor for the inequality of social relationships.[9] But, how does Leñero manage to adapt the formula to elaborate an examination of the working environment in the Distrito Federal? The structure of *Los albañiles* is that of a detective novel, but the other elements of the formula are betrayed in more than one sense: first, because at the end we lack a solution that allows good to triumph over evil and order over chaos; and second, because Leñero takes advantage of the hasty, contradictory testimonies to depict the tension within a specific salaried urban group.

Tzvetan Todorov[10] argued that the thriller is convincing and attractive because it allows the enigmatic coordinates to explain themselves based on intellectual, rather than magical, arguments. Based on this theory, Ricardo Szmetan, in an article appearing in the magazine *Confluencia*[11] about the detective aspect of *Los albañiles,* analyzes the novel's elements and concludes that it is in keeping with the detective genre: it has a detective, one or more guilty parties and a victim; the crime is committed for personal reasons and not professionally; the relationship between Isidro and don Jesús, with its homosexual overtones and authoritarian character, albeit ambivalent, includes amorous elements despite the inability to determine whether these were murder motives; the guilty party or parties are of paramount importance in the book; and the plot attempts to develop rationally, not based on fantastic or oneiric justifications. Simpson argues that the introduction of paradoxes and uncertainty in the text, like the collection of perspectives *á la* Rashomon, converts the novel into type of direct descendent of the nouveau roman.

It is interesting that, unlike the flow of detective literature in Mexico, in *Los albañiles* the writer does not challenge the national police, nor does he describe their corruption. His literary objective is truth, without hitches or obstacles, a social, not individual, truth.

Leñero himself made a theatrical adaptation in 1969, only five years after the novel's first edition.[12] His conclusion is substantially different: Munguía, at the end, blames the six suspects for a sort of collective crime similar to Agatha Christie's *Murder on the Orient Express.* In *Vivir del teatro,* a collection of reflections on his activity and experiences as a playwright, the writer says: "I thought I had found a dramatic structure for *Los albañiles* that would allow me to transfer some of the formal findings from the novel to the theater. In accordance with my criteria from then, most Mexican realist theater pieces had been lead into a dead end with their rigid, conventional format."[13] The writer's aspiration is to bestow an allegorical twist upon the character of Jesús (does his name bear significance?), converting his death into an object of religious immolation, a sort of sacramental rite. The end of the novel, then, is substantially more satisfying because it is shaken by allegories that simultaneously simplify and manipulate interpretations.

If *Los albañiles* is to be understood as a literary meditation on the culture and psychology of the construction worker in the capital, then *Asesinato* is a chronicle, a journalistic testimony. It is, Leñero assures, a "report or novel without fiction—and perhaps without literature—," a sort of documental collective history. Accordingly, the section "Explanations and gratitudes" opens: "In an effort to maintain the maximum degree of objectivity, all of the information throughout this book has documental support that has been made public in some manner or somehow been stated in writing of various forms. The author has tried not to take any liberties in imagining, inventing, or deducing facts; nor has he utilized material originating in interviews or personal investigations that have not been guaranteed by written proof. Only information existing in documents or public testimonies is used in this history, to avoid any suspicion of defamation or deformation of events and people conflicting with the descriptive intentions of the investigation."[14]

We are, then, presented with a scientific investigation at the hands of a novelist. The theme? A scandalous incident at 1535 Paseo de las Palmas, an upper-class neighborhood in northern Mexico City, in October 1978. Gilberto Flores Muñoz, director of the National Sugar Industry Commission, seventy-two years old, who had previously been the governor of the state of Nayarit, secretary of agriculture during the Adolfo Ruiz Cortínez regime (1952–58), and a potential presidential candidate one term later, was murdered with a machete. His cadaver was found next to that of his wife, Asunción Izquierdo de Flores Muñoz, seventy-five, a writer under the pen name of A. Izquierdo Albina and the pseudonyms Alba Sandoiz and Ana Mairena, who, with her novel *Los extraordinarios* (which, curiously, contains a scene with stabbed cadavers) had been a finalist for the Premio Biblioteca Breve de España in 1960, only four years after Leñero's triumph.

The goal of the text: to utilize the death of the Flores Muñozes to illuminate significant aspects of Mexican society in the second half of the twentieth century. There are photographs of each of the protagonists, the crime scene, the servants and the chauffeurs, the friends of the suspect, the penitentiary where the suspect is held, and even of the Mexico City newspapers (*La Prensa, Ovaciones,* and others) that covered the story. Everything seems to indicate that Leñero's function is merely to organize the information, but it is precisely at that level where the detective elements flourish: in the beginning, the newspaper headlines are shown, then various suspects are discussed, the biography of the victims, the architecture of the estate, and the various clues. Then a feasible, although "debatable" conclusion is reached: the murderer was the grandson, Gilberto "Quile" Flores Alavéz, whose motives could range from inheritance to hostility toward the character of his grandparents or even mental illness.

At the same time, the author introduces the character of Jesús Miyazawa Alvarez, then the director of the Policia Judicial del Distrito, and some of the experts from the Procuraduría de Justicia and the División de Investigaciones. As the years pass, the truth behind the case not only remains elusive, but starts becoming chaotic. As in *Los albañiles,* the novel is an exhaustive search for details, although here reality, not imagination, is judged.

As the testimony unfolds, chaos and untruth are propagated. "The Murder Novel," the book's fourth part, is dedicated to explaining the multiple contradictions surrounding the case. It is deduced, for example, that Gilberto Flores Alavéz's luck was spent. Political machinations used him because he had bought some machetes to demolish a shack and that, whether he were responsible or not, pointed toward his guilt, along with the trails of blood, the gloves, and the raincoat. When he was indicted and sentenced to twenty-eight years in jail, the public seemed satisfied, but not Leñero, because, as the facts are revealed, other possibilities (proposed by the defense) became feasible and the novelist addresses them. In one, for example, two assailants could have penetrated the mansion, perhaps through the garden door, and could have used Gilberto's machetes, motivated by some political vengeance against the sugar director.

Asesinato is composed of reports, quotes, letters in newspapers that support Quile, missives to president José López Portillo that remained unanswered, articles, and descriptions. The book concludes with a 1984 interview by Leñero himself and the journalist Oscar Hinojosa of Quile in his cell. Nothing is resolved; the mystery remains without an irrefutable explanation.

In addition to utilizing journalistic techniques to construe an aggregation of Mexican motives, rivalries, and dishonesty, Leñero is also interested in demonstrating how prison in the Distrito Federal is a paradise for the wealthy and living hell for the poor. When the writer finds himself with Quile in his cell in the Reclusorio Oriente, he discovers he has all the comforts of the privileged: stereo, comfortable room, pressed clothing. Thus, there are two messages: one, that politics so influence daily events at every level that everything is dirty and corrupt; and two, that justice is not an egalitarian solution to infractions of the law and moral requisites, implying that jail is not a punishment, and the guilty do not pay for their sins. In this sense Leñero goes further than Helú, Martínez de la Vega, or Usigli because while they leave a crime unpunished, in *Asesinato* the criminal pays, although without a sufficiently arduous lesson, sanction, or penitence.

It would not be inaccurate to argue that Leñero's work is based on the techniques and elements of the detective novel, but with the aim to demonstrate Mexico's immorality and to investigate society as a whole. To Caillois's question, "Who?" he answers: Everyone and no one is to blame, and it is impossible to prove otherwise. His narrative maneuvers allude to "anti-deduction" in the way suspense, detection, and explanation function to immerse themselves—in real or invented cases—in the hidden veins of Mexican idiosyncracy. Ultimately, the reader ends up at once disillusioned and satisfied: disillusioned, because human reason is fallible and does not triumph over darkness; satisfied, because beyond the truth, society is studied at a global level and from many perspectives. Leñero, then, borrows certain elements from the tradition of Agatha Christie or Conan Doyle to serve his own epistemological interests, nothing more; he cares little about respecting, in a dogmatic sense, the detective standards.

19

Jorge Ibargüengoitia

Born in Guanajuato in 1928, Jorge Ibargüengoitia, whose family moved to the Distrito Federal when he was thirteen, studied engineering at the Universidad Nacional Autónoma de México, but abandoned this notion and returned home to work on a ranch. After three years in the province, he decided to dedicate himself to the theater after one of *Los Contemporáneos*, Salvador Novo, director of the Teatro Juárez, presented *Rosalba y los llaveros,* a play by Emilio Carballido. Novo invited Ibargüengoitia to one of the performances, and the episode enchanted the young man. "I don't know if the performance was excellent or if my anemic condition was extraordinarily receptive," Ibargüengoitia later would recall. "The truth is that I know now, and confess with a little embarrassment, that no theatrical performance has affected me like that *Rosalba y los llaveros* I saw at Teatro Juárez . . . I said: no more ranch!, and at that moment I was no longer a farmhand. Three months later I enrolled in the Facultad de Folosofia y Letras."[1]

At the university he met Rodolfo Usigli, who was then teaching a course on the theory of theatrical composition. His relationship with the author of *Crown of Shadows* became tight. The young playwright wrote a few theatrical pieces for Usigli and later more on his own, only a handful of which were ever performed.

With one, *El atentado,* based on the assassination of General Alvaro Obregón, he won the Cuban Casa de las Américas theater prize in 1963. In an article in *Vuelta* from 1985, he said: "*El atentado* left me with two impressions: it closed the doors to the theater for me and opened those of the novel. When I was doing research for this piece I found material that made me conceive the idea of writing a novel about the last part of the Mexican Revolution."[2] The investigation inspired him to write *Lightning in August* (1964), and years later, *Los pasos de López* (1982). He died tragically in an aerial accident in Barajas, Madrid, in 1983, along with Uruguayan critic Angel Rama, Peruvian novelist Manuel Scorza, and Argentine writer and art critic Marta Traba.

His literary career started to gain momentum as a columnist and theater critic in *Excélsior, Vuelta, Siempre!, Diálogos,* and the *Revista de la Universidad de México,* followed by six novels and volumes of stories. Two novels in particular display an appreciable affiliation with the detective genre: *The Dead Girls*[3] and *Two Crimes.*[4]

The former, one of his most celebrated works, is set in the Bajío. It is about a pair of matrons and their prostitutes, known as Las Poquianchis, and is based on an actual event which took place between 1963 and 1964 in San Francisco del Rincón. It was a scandalous incident that was reported in every paper and by all the news media and was later made into a film, *Las Poquianchis,* directed by Felipe Cazals in 1977. Octavio Paz, who rarely writes about novels, perhaps for a lack of respect for fictitious narration due to his poetic bent,[5] wrote in his *Sombras de Obras :*

> The story Ibargüengoitia tells us is not only unrealistic, despite being real, but seems incredible. *The Dead Girls* brings up the traditional theme of the surrealism of reality once more. It is the *par excellence* novelistic theme, the same question that went unanswered by Cervantes and Dickens, Balzac and Joyce: are the windmills giants or windmills? Ibargüengoitia's novel is more a variation of the eternal theme, the first and the last, the true and only theme of literary art: the essentially mysterious nature of human beings. In the art of the novel the question of reality or surrealism of reality is presented as a description of the area where it is difficult to tell bad from good, crime from innocence. That uncertainty, which is what makes men what they are, is that which gives reality to the atrocious surrealism of *The Dead Girls.*[6]

Ibargüengoitia undertook this project following *Estas ruinas que ves* (1979). It is set in Cuévano, a fictitious province, the author's invented geography which appears in many of his books, which could be compared to Guanajuato; the anonymous protagonist, an autobiographical semblance, is also a maestro of literature writing a book about matrons who murdered their prostitutes. It is, then, a sort of roman à clef.

In the novel, a matron and her partner kill a gang of prostitutes when their economic situation makes it impossible to keep supporting them. Jorge Ibargüengoitia bases the plot on a real story but cautions in an introductory note: "Some of the incidents recounted here are real. All of the characters are imagined."[7] The narration is semi-documental, a juxtaposition of facts and fantasy. It opens when three men and a woman arrive at a town, looking for a Simón Corona, a baker, to settle a score. When they find him, they shoot him, douse the establishment with gasoline, and set it on fire.

Simón somehow survives and reports Serafina Baladro, an old lover, to the police. Later, the two are accused of a crime from 1960; a conspiracy is gradually exposed in which Serafina and her sister Arcángela Baladro (a name fashioned in Gabriel García Márquez's literary universe?) murdered and buried some young women, whom they had converted into prostitutes. Things become complicated because Serafina has a romantic relationship with Capitán Bedoya (a name alluding to *Treasure of Sierra Madre* by B. J. Traven), who protects her and indirectly participates in the criminal events. His corruption and lack of legal thoroughness only serve to further entangle the proceedings.

Inspector Teódulo Cueto maintains a certain complicity with the Baladro sisters in the way he approaches the keys to the mystery, and manipulates the system to protect the criminals. Finally, the moment of truth comes, and the bodies are found: there is a stinking odor in the Casino del Danzón, next to the Rancho de los Angeles, where the matrons brought the prostitutes after the authorities closed their establishment for threatening the respectability of the citizenry. Ultimately, all of the details are so shocking that not even the journalistic tone can counteract the sense of improbability discussed by Paz.

Ibargüengoitia's technical choice of the chronicle is significant in how it limits the spontaneity of fiction and circumscribes reality. The style is very similar to that of another contemporary novel, *The Truth about the Savolta Case* (1975) by the Spaniard Eduardo Mendoza,[8] which recreates the confrontation between workers and their employers and the revolutionary tension in Barcelona from 1917 to 1919, which in turn harkens, albeit in a veiled manner, to the polyphonic structure of Collins's *The Moonstone*. Mendoza juxtaposes photostatic facsimiles of *La voz de la justicia*, a Barcelona newspaper of the era, stenographic notes, interviews, police letters and files, third-person narrations, and so on. The result is a 463-page mosaic, in Seix-Barral's Biblioteca de Bolsillo edition, where fiction mingles with journalism, truth with lies.

Ibargüengoitia, as Paz attested, undertakes a similar task. In *The Dead Girls* there are medical reports and interviews. There are also copies of documents, archive files, and recorded testimony. The segments, whatever their origin, are juxtaposed so they maintain suspense and reveal facts slowly and deliberately. The writer's task is not just to utilize real events to prove their "unrealness." It is also to prove that the fallibility of justice reigns in Mexico and it is here where the detective metabolism enters the scene: for example, there is a detective (Teódulo Cueto) who handles the case despite his incompetence, there are various criminals and accomplices who should be brought to justice, although we doubt they will pay for their crimes, and there is suspense.

To address Caillois's questions, the writer is interested, if not in the *who,* then in the *how, why, when,* and *where* of the Baladro sisters' abuses. The novel is far from an example of classic detective literature. The reader visits the events, not from the inspector's perspective (who is involved through chapter 16) but that of the prostitutes and their matron, through public information.

Compared with the author's previous works, here there is less humor, although there is satire in the way Ibargüengoitia assumes the narrative voice. His main interest lies in depicting society while maintaining faith to the different voices, documents, and police notes. The setting, like in *Maten al león,* is geographically fictitious: the city of Pedrones, the state of Plan de Abajo, Salto de Tuxpana, the state of Mezcala, Muérdago, San Pedro de las Corrientes, and so on. The narration is converted into a parodical concert of voices and ghosts where the entire community is the protagonist. The legal complications and the narrative movement from one locality to another open the literary range.

In "Memorias de novelas," an article in *Autopsias rápidas,* a volume of his essays edited by Guillermo Sheridan, Ibargüengoitia says:

> Towards the end of 1964 I made a disorganized investigation of the Las Poquianchis case and wrote a folder of some one hundred pages that is neither a report, essay, nor novel, which I did not like when I finished and did not serve any purpose. In 1965 I decided that I should write a novel based on it. In 1970 I worked a few months towards this end; "working" at that time consisted of sitting in front of a desk with a blank sheet of paper and then falling asleep on the couch and waiting until an idea struck me. After much work I produced some hundred fifty pages that I later threw out . . . To uncover information was not an easy thing, because one could write another book even more scandalous than the one I wrote about the lies issued by the press and the truths they forgot. The legal dossier has more than a thousand pages, office-sized, both sides single-spaced. Some of the deponents had more than four given names—A, alias B or C, also known as D—, others are presented with three pairs of last names; on the other hand nobody could remember the name of one of the victims. I read the newspapers and part of the dossier, but I did not interview any of the protagonists.[9]

The detective skeleton is used, but good does not prevail. The structure is similar to Leñero's *Asesinato* at two levels: one, it plays with the text-document, offering objective testimonies never hindered by a narrative voice; and second, the prison finale is similar because in *The Dead Girls,* the sisters, Serafina and Arcángela, although in jail, maintain their lifestyles selling refreshments at exorbitant prices and loaning money. The difference, clearly, is that all the characters in *The Dead Girls* are fictitious, the author's inventions, and his apparent objectivity is only that, an appearance. Furthermore, Ibargüengoitia's goal is not only to illustrate Mexico's moral fiber without intrusion, but to do so through jokes and comedy. When the time comes to discover the inhumations, for example, he makes the detective walk over the common grave, not knowing from where the fetid odor of decomposing flesh is originating, even when the ground is soft and crumbly. Or he abuses feminine ingenuousness by making the prostitutes an involuntary, dumb pack, easily manipulated by the Baladro sisters and for no apparent reason. The author gracefully describes it all without excessive seriousness, like one who smiles facing a catastrophe.

Other Ibargüengoitia novels also use crime and investigation. For instance, *Maten al león* starts with the 1926 assassination of Dr. Saldaña, an opposition candidate on the fictitious Caribbean island of Arepa. An investigation is ordered, but clearly, from the start, everyone knows that it was the dictator and absolute ruler, Belaunzarán, who ordered the murder.[10]

Ibargüengoitia frequently discussed detective themes in articles published in *Excélsior* and *Vuelta,* which Sheridan assembled into a Vuelta publishing house collection and into two volumes published by Joaquín Mortiz. "Homage to James Bond" ("Homenaje a James Bond")[11] and "Agatha Christie: An Unlikely Obituary" ("Resuélvame este caso") stand out[12]; this paragraph comes from the former.

The difference between a normal novel and a detective story is that the former is, or pretends to be, a living organism, while the latter is, and knows that it is, a mechanism. The serious writer is presenting a view of the world as he sees it, while the writer of thrillers is constructing something that resembles life and is just a series of interesting situations that happen to imaginary character, who is everything that most people would want to be and are not. For instance, James Bond arrives in Munich and knows where he can eat the best *liverwurst* in the city. At a certain point he says, "I fancy a *schnapps.*" That is to say, he is a gentleman always knowing what he wants, how to get it, and always having the money to pay for it. Let's imagine James Bond entering a restaurant and not knowing what to opt for, the table in the hallway, or the one in the corner. That of course, would be the end of the Secret Service. However, no doubt it happens to us all once in a while.

Ibargüengoitia, again with humor, proceeds to praise the superhero attributes of the British spy: his gorgeous women, physical prowess, and moral integrity. And at the end of the article he asks, "I guess what I'm trying to say is: Why don't we Mexicans do something like that? Why don't we write books glorifying our secret service?"[13]

The second article says:

> In the last few weeks three different people have asked why didn't I write an obituary for Agatha Christie or an article about her under the pretext of her death. I told all three the same thing: that to me, this woman's books seem unreadable, because the ones I read or tried to read, have caused one of two experiences for me: I have found out who the murderer was on page 40, because of my own intuition for which she isn't to blame (for instance, I think that if a gentleman's only characteristic is that he winds all the clocks in the house everyday, he must be the criminal); or, on the contrary, I finish the novel not knowing which way is up, and I can't understand the explanation Poirot gives at the end, so I'm totally confused. But this mundane and contemptuous attitude is, on second thought, false. I think what actually happens to me with Agatha Christie, and with any detective story in which I have to solve a mystery, is that I'm a total failure.[14]

Ibargüengoitia protests the detective novel and in the next few paragraphs jokes about certain objects that disappeared from his house in his childhood or during a recent dinner party he and his wife threw, and solves the puzzle in an extremely jocular, anti-detective manner. These texts shed light on Ibargüengoitia's attitude toward the presence of detective art in everyday Mexican life from the seventies on. Although the author resists subscribing to the tradition, it is more than likely that his readings, visits to the movies, and television programs have penetrated him, at least subconsciously. *The Dead Girls*, among others, is an example of that penetration. Just like *Los albañiles* by Leñero—who, incidentally, wrote *Los pasos de Jorge*, published by Joaquín Mortiz in 1989, a book which establishes a chronology of the life and works of Ibargüengoitia and refers to his relationship with his university tutor, Rodolfo Usigli—is a demonstration of how the "subgenre" inhabits everyday life, metamorphosing and disguising itself. From a commercial point of view, an author like Ibargüengoitia knows that thrillers sell and stimulate the imagination (his and the next person's). Thus, when he sits to write, its shadow inevitably pursues and possesses him.

Two Crimes is a more traditional, less successful, novel. It contains the same humor. Its motivating force, less ambitious than other works, is the illustration of provincial customs. Ibargüengoitia was proposing to create a "light-hearted piece like Graham Greene (*Our Man in Havana*) in his more serious novels."[15] Many consider it a masterpiece.[16] Once again, the work has an autobiographical bent: it involves a nephew's inheritance from an uncle (which Ibargüengoitia received between 1952 and 1953) and about the adventures of a one-time engineering student.[17] The plot unfolds in Muérdago, state of Plan de Abajo.

The narration is divided into two parts: the first is narrated by the protagonist, Marcos "Negro" González. He recounts how, after a night of partying, drinking, and taking cocaine at his house, he escapes from the police, who violate the Constitution by entering without permission. Eager for money, González comes to the town of Muérdago, where his rich uncle, Ramón Tarragona, lives. Trying, like his cousins, to get his hands on his uncle's fortune, he provokes a family controversy. González starts romantic affairs with his cousin, Amalia, and with Lucero, Amalia's daughter. Passing himself off as a graduated metallurgical engineer, he convinces his uncle to invest in some abandoned mines a few minutes outside town.

In the second part, the narrator is an improvised detective, the pharmacist José Lara, one of Tarragona's friends. "What I am about to tell is the only notable thing that has happened in my life," says Lara in chapter 9. "After fifty years as an apothecary, I became a detective. I can't say that I triumphed in this second capacity, but I fared better than the professionals who intervened in the case I was trying to solve."[18] He recounts how Tarragona, after giving González a check for 40,000 pesos, in addition to amending his will to include his nephew, is poisoned and dies. The cousins blame González, but Marcos had also been poisoned, and as there is no proof, he inherits his share. After the testamentary proceedings, the transfer of goods is coupled with a picnic and hunt. Suspense reigns. Are they planning to kill the "Negro"? All of a sudden, someone carrying González's poncho is gunned down. It is Lucero: she dies after mistaking the criminal, believing she was killing the fraudulent cousin.

From the preceding description, one can infer that there are murders, detectives, and humor, and that information reaches us gradually. Once again Ibargüengoitia utilizes only the elements of the formula that suit him. The testimony coming from Lara is that of an amateur private eye. His logic is neither detailed nor deductive. However, he objectively explains the details of the first and second murders because he is close to the family and he has the necessary information to examine poisonous substances. His investigation and González's narration are delivered with an uninhibited, humorous tone. The novel is at the midpoint between Helú and Bermúdez, and Paco Ignacio Taibo II and *The Dead Girls*. It subscribes to neither the British nor North American models because Ibargüengoitia's primary objective is to illustrate the customs and intellectual limitations of the *provincianos* through two murders.

It is apparent that the author of *The Dead Girls* and *Two Crimes* maintained only an irreverent, ludic affiliation with the detective novel and that he took advantage of its mechanisms to illustrate, with a smile, the social composition of the Mexican province.

20

José Emilio Pacheco

Perhaps the most experimental and "open" detective novel within Mexican literature is *Morirás lejos*.[1] Its author, José Emilio Pacheco, was born in Mexico in 1939. He is a poet, narrator, essayist, anthologist, and translator of T. S. Eliot and Oscar Wilde, among others. He boasts three collections of stories, *La sangre de Medusa* (1958) *El viento distante* (1963), and *El principio del placer* (1972). His 1981 novella *Batallas en el desierto*, included in *Battles in the Desert & Other Stories,* is an exposé of the Distrito Federal in the sixties, from the perspective of a middle-class child in the Condesa suburb who falls in love with his best friend's mother.

Morirás lejos, a novel with a "secret" affiliation with the detective genre, begins with what Henry James calls a *showing:* from his window, eme, the protagonist, observes an unknown person (later called Alguien, or "someone")[2] seated on a park bench, reading the classified ads in *El Universal.* Nothing happens. What is more, we know upon closing the text that only a few seconds occur in "real time," although we have been through, in "narrative time," a total of 154 pages of history, anguish, and descriptions. But the plot has a flip-side: eme is not watching, it is he who is being watched, his guilt wears him down and he senses he will be the target of some conspiracy. As readers, we want to know who has committed the crime, when, why, how, and where.

I previously mentioned that the success of a detective novel depends upon the meticulous management of information and secrets, which are gradually disclosed from many different angles through a dialectic of oppositions. I commented in chapter 1 that this opposition of progress and regress has been utilized by the Russian formalists who distinguish between motifs essential to the disentanglement of the plot and dispensable motifs.[3] I have also mentioned that the detective genre is like a coherent, linear, and conservative presentation of facts, and that it rejects that which is unconventional and stylistic devices, preferring cold logic and established guidelines, which attests to its "legibility."[4]

Moriras Lejos breaks from this legibility by using an antitraditional discourse technique, implying it is like literary experimentation. Furthermore, it has an atypical distribution of characters; atypical and mannequin-like, because morality never triumphs. Not to mention the alternation of perspective; Pacheco uses narrators who seem omniscient yet are involved in the plot, but this strategy results in an ambiguous ending. The voice which narrates the chapters subtitled "Salónica" is in first person, sometimes singular and other times plural; the remainder, the history of the Jews from the destruction of the Second Temple in Jerusalem, recounted by Josephus Flavius, through the Nazi holocaust ("Diaspora" and "Grossaktion"), utilizes one voice in third person alternating with a medley of testimonies like Ludwig Hirshfeld's, annotations from the diary of Hans Frank, and orders from Heinrich Himmler, among other things.

"Salónica" is disquieting because the omniscient narrator's level of involvement is constantly fluctuating. The initial *showing* is seen from a distance, with a certain impartiality, but is occasionally confusing, as in line 29: "Let us insist: riddles are not a game."[5] This *let us insist* would seem to be a conventional form of reference, common in scientific and rhetorical writing. But the indubitable refutation of this theory appears further along, in lines 41 and 42 of the same chapter: "the faith in his own power, that characterized, unfortunately for us, the eme we all knew."[6] The *our* prompts suspicion that the narrator (and perhaps the reader) has been an acquaintance of eme, who knows him and perhaps shares a history. Both syntactical choices could also mean that the narrator and the reader constitute an inseparable narrative voice, a *we*, and in that respect there is a metatextual link.

If such a metatextual bond exists, what function does it serve? The theories of reception by Hans Robert Jauss, Wolfgang Iser, and Umberto Eco may be helpful. In *Morirás lejos* there does not exist, as in Cortázar's *Hopscotch* (Rayuela), a classification of "female reader" (who understands only the explicit meaning) and the "complicit reader" (who understands both implicit and explicit meanings). Pacheco addresses only one type of reader: active, who can produce the entire novelistic scheme. Wolfgang Iser, in *The Implicit Reader* and *The Act of Reading*,[7] discusses the reader whose position changes in accordance with the "blanks" within the text. For him, a novel is only meaningful through omissions, rather than blunt affirmations to endow form and weight to the content.

Unlike the typical detective novel, in *Morirás lejos* we know who is pursued but not who is chasing. We would abandon the genre if we were to accept that eme is paranoid and that the person watching him is, and will remain, unknown. But Iser's theory is appropriate because Pacheco renounces the easy escape and offers the following list of solutions:

a) the stranger is a worker looking for work;
b) he is a sexual delinquent who stalks his victim;
c) he is a father who has lost his child and is looking for where he spent his life;
d) he is the lover of a woman who will pass through the park;
e) he is a nostalgic individual who spent his early years in the park;
f) he is a hallucination because nobody is sitting on the bench;
g) he is a private investigator who has been hired to write a report on some person;
h) the park does not exist;
i) eme does not exist because he died during World War II;
j) the person waiting by the window is not eme;
k) the city does not exist;
l) the window blinds are closed;
m) there is enough information to choose only one alternative;
n) everything *Morirás lejos* says is true;
ñ) there is a couple sitting on the park bench;
o) the house where eme supposedly is was demolished in 1959;
p) the development of the alternatives is wasted time because it always refers to different books;
q) someone enjoys imagining;
r) the options offered between *m* and *p* are absurd;
s) the stranger is murmuring something;
t) the initial situation is restored;
u) it is a frustrated playwright;
v) an enthusiastic writer looking for work;
y) all of the above information should be entered into a computer;
z) the stranger performs adjectivable behavior in every previous option;[8]

The options can be divided into those implausible and those feasible; *h* separates the real from the unreal because starting there, with the exception of *u* and *v*, no answer is provided as to the pursuer's identity. "The hypotheses may be infinite,"[9] but the alphabet, which is the *rational* list of letters used daily, limits them; we ought to fill in the "blanks" that resolve the enigma of identity.

In *Lector in fabula*,[10] Eco proposes other useful terms: the differentiation between the text's narrative world and the "possible worlds," the "inferential walk" or the "ghost chapters" that the text inspires in the reader. Beyond the written novel there is one unwritten, submerged, which allows the reader to contribute to the creative process, ordering, negotiating, and constructing, to apply his own vision.

Along with Iser and Eco's ideas, that of Hans Robert Jauss should be considered, which, in *Aesthetic Experience and Literary Hermeneutics,*[11] views the work of art as defined by two vectors: by its reading through time, which can vary according to the reader's experience, familiarity, and expectations; and by how a novel's reading can enter into a reader's life (the classic example is *Don Quixote,* which, while parodying the scope of the chivalric novel, extends those boundaries toward other worlds). According to Jauss, Iser, and Eco, it is we, each individual reader, in collaboration with the narrator, who assume the role of the detective.

A note on page 45 (added in the 1977 edition) reads: "Who is the omniscient narrator? One of the two: eme or the man seated fourteen or fifteen meters from the well with '*El aviso oportuno*' in his hands." This affirmation is similar to the literary act of autobiography in third person; in other words, either eme or the stranger, each a player within the scene, also lives outside it. But the role of the metatextual association remains intact: if the stranger or eme are, in effect, the voice of that omniscient narrator, the narrative voice has become out of phase with one of the characters, without dismantling the triptych of "eme," "stranger," and "narrator."

The range of possibilities within the text depends upon the stylistic technique. The writer chooses the conditional to allow alternatives. For example: "of the line eme *could* see between the blinds."[12] The combination attracts uncertainty: Why is eme where he is? What is his crime? Who is he? But the answers are slow to arrive (or they never do), and although the conditional, the *could,* entails its negation (e.g., *could not*), we do not know if the narrative metabolism is inclined toward affirmation or negation. The purpose of the conditional is again insinuated in the aforementioned lines from the first chapter: "Let us insist: riddles are not game: it deals with an enigma initiated one afternoon in 1946 or 1947."[13] The three terms, "riddle," "enigma," and "game," invite deduction but lack the rigor found in the novels of Agatha Christie or Arthur Conan Doyle for the simple reason that, in Pacheco's novel, the reader is the key figure, for example, Hercule Poirot or Sherlock Holmes.

The detective characteristic of *Morirás lejos* is the labyrinthine, persistent, baroque suspense. That detective suspense results in the clarification of Caillois's questions: *who* is eme? An ex-Nazi doctor who formed part of the *Geheime Staatpolizei* and, like Joseph Mengele, committed atrocities in German laboratories with civilians, especially twins and pregnant women, and managed to escape after World War II had ended. Pacheco deindividualizes the character and converts him into an archetype by utilizing a phenomenon instead of a patronymic (the exercise is common in the French and Central European literature of Duras, Kafka, Kundera, and others). The letter "m" is chosen because eme could be, among other things: evil (*mal*), dead (*muerte*), *mauet, meurtrier, macabre, malediction, menace, mis á mort, mischung, mancherlei, mauchelrond, maskenazung, marchen, messerheld, minaccia, miragio, macello, massacro*.[14] All of these possibilities are suggested by Pacheco. Eme is, then, evil (*el mal*), the force that disorganizes nature. The remainder of the questions—how, where, when, and why—become clear upon understanding the character's infamy and psychology, and the historical setting where he committed his criminal acts.

Just like in "Las babas del diablo" by Julio Cortázar, *Morirás lejos* elaborates a profound meditation on narrative art. But unlike the Argentine's text, he does not place a perceptive-epistemological paradigm at the core. Rather, he investigates the possibilities of deduction. He investigates them to infinity because the stranger "is condemned to spend the rest of the days and years of his life before eme, to sit on the bench smelling of vinager, the same section of *El Universal* in his hands; so eme senses him and looks at him as a pursuer—at him, so far removed from eme's past—and occupies his free time, his seclusion, his fear, with deductions no longer brilliant nor original."[15]

In fact, we are also condemned to attempt a temporal, ephemeral solution, one that cannot be included in future editions. *Morirás lejos* is a detective anti-novel where good does not triumph and one's intellect is diverted, exploring its own limits. More than a mere pastime, it is a map of the fallible and open universe of rationality. We are the detectives but there is no solution. We know who is guilty and why, but there is no way to apprehend him. It is, then, converted into a laboratory of possibilities. Within its pages it summarizes any other detective novel and simultaneously denies it.

Appendix
Interview with Paco Ignacio Taibo II

IS: When and how did you begin to write?*

PIT II: When I first learned how to form my letters, the moment I acquired the use of reason. Since then, writing has been my destiny. At age eleven, I was making steps toward printing a magazine, and at thirteen, I wrote my first short story. I have been a journalist since age fifteen, an obsessive reader since five, and I managed to finish my first novel, which fortunately was never published, at twenty. I suppose that this obsession is part of a family tradition nurtured by a great uncle who was also a writer, and by my father, Paco Ignacio Taibo, a journalist, novelist, and critic according to whom the best trade of the world wasn't to be a trapeze artist or a fireman—those are no doubt the best secondary trades—but a writer. When I was five years old, my father used to come home from the newspaper for which he worked, in the middle of the night, and instead of going to bed, he would put newspapers and a towel on the dining room table and over them his Olivetti typewriter. He would then write a novel trying to make as little noise as possible in order not to wake up the family. He would write until dawn. I would silently escape from bed and crawl beneath the table. It was very clear to me that my father was doing something very important, so important that I had to be a witness . . . I slept the first years of my life lulled by an Olivetti.

IS: What technique do you follow? What schedule? Do you have any talisman that inspires you warding off evil spirits?

PIT II: I write all day at all hours. I tend to work with music—the more rhythmic, the better. Richard Wagner and Carlos Santana, for example. My only talisman is a change of work. I am a voracious writer. It could be that right now I have begun three novels, another three are outlined with notes, a historical essay about Mexican anarchists of the twenties, two or three reports, and a comic-strip script. I go from one text to another. When I feel that I am not getting anywhere with one project, I abandon it and begin another. I tend to have a few dry spells and when

Mexico City, June 1991. First published in *La Nueva España* (Oviedo), no. 131 (5 July 1991): 35–36. Translated into English by Carrie Van Doren in *The Literary Review*, vol. 38, no. 1 (Fall 1994): 34–37; reprinted by permission of the editors.

they arrive I don't fight them, but rather, I travel and dedicate myself to helping here and there in community projects.

IS: What was your first encounter with Héctor Belascoarán Shayne? Where does his physical appearance and his intellectual capacity come from?

PIT II: He was born by elimination and his physical presence developed from a variety of things. He is rootless, a refugee of the middle class, madly curious, stubborn, full of humorous feeling toward his fellow Mexicans, a bit melancholic. Actually, his appearance came from an anthropologist friend, Sergio Perelló, who wore the clothing of the fashion fifteen years ago. Belascoarán Shayne has become what he is over fifteen years of backwardness. I should also add that his appearance was formed from injuries and wounds throughout the novels: the loss of an eye, a slight limp, the horror of humidity which makes his bones grind.

IS: Arthur Conan Doyle, tired of his character Sherlock Holmes, once killed him, only to bring him back later on upon the petitioning of his readers. Belascoarán Shayne seems also to have been resuscitated in your novel *Regreso a la misma ciudad y bajo la lluvia?* Does he control you or vice versa?

PIT II: We control each other. I didn't kill him, dramatic logic killed him, the progression of facts. Then the readers protested. I decided that the saga wasn't finished and revived it. White magic!

IS: What is the relationship between Belascoarán Shayne and Phillip Marlowe? What are their differences?

PIT II: The differences are in the structure of the lone hero, the outsider: a vocation for solitude, a fidelity to friends (in Marlowe's case) and to certain obsessions (in Belascoarán Shayne's case). Raymond Chandler's character moves within rational histories whereas mine is surrounded by a chaotic atmosphere, Kafkaesque and corrupt: Mexico City.

IS: To what do you attribute your huge popularity?

PIT II: To exoticism . . . I suppose Mexican readers find in my novels a broken mirror, a proposition that invites them not to surrender to an immoral reality.

IS: Why is detective fiction so attractive?

PIT II: Because of the allure of adventure, the virtues of enigma, an incredible capacity for discovering cities and ancient mysteries, a set of characters in limited situations. A good novel is a good novel, but if it has a detective plot, all the better.

IS: Before you, the Mexican detective novel didn't subscribe to the dirty realism of Chandler, Dashiell Hammett, and Ernest Hemingway. How come? Why this new affiliation?

PIT II: In reality, I subscribe to the Ugly-Dirty-Fucking Realism of Chester Himes and Jim Thomson, in the worst sense of the word—that of storytellers. I have added to this black humor and a Kafka-style twist in morality. I feel identified with a generation of narrators who wrote in the same years as I and see literature as subversive subversion: Manuel Vásquez Montalbán, Jerome Charyn, J. P. Manchette, Jean Francois Vilar, Juan Carlos Martelli, Alberto Sperati, Per Wahloo, Robert Littell, Martin Cruz-Smith; likewise, with a current trend of writers of nonfiction testimonies: Rodolfo Walsh, Miguel Bonasso, Joseph Wambaugh, and Guillermo Thorndyke.

IS: Do you consider María Elvira Bermúdez, Antonio Helú, Pepe Martínez de la Vega, and Rafael Solana your Mexican precursors, all writers who wrote detective stories from the thirties to the fifties south of the Rio Grande, although in a very different way? What do you think of Rafael Bernal's *El complot mongol*?

PIT II: I don't think of them as precursors. I don't owe them anything, nor do I want to maintain relations with a generation of parodists and imitators. Their books interest me little and their approximation of style is spineless. The only work that attracts me is Bernal, which has been unfairly forgotten and which my generation has somehow revived.

IS: What do you think of Jorge Ibargüengoitia's *The Dead Girls* and Vicente Leñero's 1967 novel *Los albañiles*, the works of two writers who reinvigorated detective fiction without ever considering themselves practitioners?

PIT II: They interest me as precursors to the nouveau detectives in Mexico and the Southern hemisphere in general. You're right: what is curious is that both authors never consider themselves part of this style.

IS: Talk to me about Carlos Fuentes' *The Hydra Head*. Also, more than about your detective, talk to me about Mexico City, which was also Fuentes' protagonist in *Where the Air is Clear*.

PIT II: I feel an affinity toward Fuentes, although not toward *The Hydra Head*. I like his novels dealing with this monstrous metropolis, a city that manages to obsess me. The city produces more stories in one day than Balzac would have been able to tell in numerous lifetimes. There is in this a perverse condensation of schizophrenia and horror, adorned in a mountain of myths, an incredible fountain of inspiration. Frankly, this place is shaky and full of bad vibrations and aloneness. It is surrounded by catastrophe, and people protest every day the miserable way of life they are forced to live in. But they don't leave. This place makes me sick: I can't manage to grasp its essence.

IS: What is there in you of Julio Cortázar? What influence if any did the Latin-American literary boom writers have on your work—Mario Vargas Llosa, Gabriel García Márquez, and José Donoso?

PIT II: I like Cortázar but I don't know . . . Something in him bothers me and keeps me away. About the rest, nothing. The first five novels of Vargas Llosa attracted me, but the rest are a bore. In fact, I feel very influenced by Antonio Skármeta, Oswaldo Soriano, Eduardo Galeano,

Jesus Díaz, writers of another generation in whose novels the need to locate a story in a historical context is essential.

IS: Mexico is a country where there is so much corruption that justice is obliterated. Is that the main theme of your national detective literature?

PIT II: Yes, that's the point. Criminality forms part of the system and is incorporated into it in a logical and coherent manner. Hence, the solution is also part of the crime. I live in a city where the police produce more deaths than all of the underworld organizations, the Mafia, and any number of marginal lunatics. Luis González de Alba, a student leader of the Tlatelolco movement of 1968, was absurdly imprisoned for four years for setting fire to a streetcar in the intersection of two streets, a place where there had never been rails, and at a time during which he was giving a lecture before thousands of witnesses on the other side of the city. To him, of course, we owe the famous phrase: "The police is always to be blamed."

Afterword

At the end of "Point of Departure," a few questions were posed: When did the detective genre penetrate Mexico? Who read these works and in what language? Who wrote the first native attempts? How did they copy the model, and what elements did they introduce to differentiate their work? Who came next? Is there a "Mexican" contribution to detective fiction? In response I have offered a study, both panoramic and analytical, of the origins, production, and impact of detective literature in Mexico. I included biographical information on each author, his context and his motivation.

I have illustrated how, starting in 1968, these novelists shook their sense of inferiority and filled the scene with detective novels, sometimes disguised, sometimes not. The tendency to look at this "subgenre" out of the corner of one's eye became passé, and the post-Tlatelolco writers embraced the notions of experimentation, creation of their own private eyes, and the use of Mexico as an ad hoc setting for such literature. Although some critics have exhibited interest, it is not always with sufficient enthusiasm, or perhaps with a negative tone, which makes one think that proper reception is still want for a certain maturation to verbalize the genre's ongoing contribution. But aside from that, readers have always supported these manifestations, whether they are "descended" from Chandler and Hammett, like Héctor Belascoarán Shayne, or when the formula becomes a ghost, a whisper, like in Vicente Leñero, José Emilio Pacheco, and Jorge Ibargüengoitia. These two directions show that in Mexico the genre is not only produced for the masses, but also for a more sophisticated audience, whose education and demands are greater.

The first manifestations appeared in the twenties, but it was not until Ensayo de un crimen that they found purchase in the mainstream. Before 1968, the British bent predominated; afterwards, it was the hard-boiled side and the revolutions inspired by the nouveau roman and Nabokov or Borges.

And the future? It is safe to say that the detective novel in Mexico is in good health and must continue to be recognized, using local jargon. Television and cinema keep eating up thrillers, not to

148

mention the flood of adaptations of Spanish works. At this moment, the detective novel has reached an apotheosis and lies in wait of a Cervantes, ready to pit his hidalgo and escudero against the diabolical forces trying to destabilize the natural order of things.

Carlos Monsivaís's assertion, then, that there is no unique detective literature in Mexico, nor is it feasible that one appear, has been proven incorrect. In a corrupt environment, where sarcasm and hypocrisy thrive and power is monopolized, there are various attitudes that the citizenry adopt before authority: apathy, ridicule, or the interpretation of its presence as a sign of iniquity. There is another alternative: based upon a detective scheme, a critical mosaic is created, where the secret veins in the depths of society are exposed. This last possibility, quite recurrent in Mexico, borrows techniques from satire and journalistic reporting. To the question, "who is to blame?" the answer is, "who isn't?" Under this banner, the detective novel flourishes in Mexico.

I have discussed traditional and experimental authors, those who have elaborated a "stylization" and those who have made a "parodical stylization," to use Bakhtin's terminology. Tlatelolco has been cited as a transition point. But even before 1968, Pepe Martínez de la Vega had already invented stories in which political corruption was the protagonist. And after, Paco Ignacio Taibo II still writes his hard-boiled novels in the spirit of the North American model.

Thanks to the likes of Fuentes, Pitol, Rafael Ramírez Heredia, Usigli, Leñero, and Bermúdez, the Distrito Federal is a "literary" metropolis. Richard Ellman once said that if Dublin were ever destroyed, it could be rebuilt based on James Joyce's *Ulysses*. Perhaps the same can be said of this motley city of Mexico, whose literary map has been the preoccupation of these writers, who have reproduced it in the geography of the imagination.

Epilogue

ANYONE well-versed in Latin American literature knows that to approach the vast, diverse panorama of twentieth-century Mexican narratives entails confronting established schemes of periodization and currents, or schools: the Mexican Revolution novel (Mariano Azuela, Martín Luis Guzmán, Agustín Yáñez, José Revueltas), the magical realism inspired by Rulfo's work, particularly *Pedro Páramo;* the copious investigative pieces on cultural roots and national identity, iniciated by Carlos Fuentes and his coterie of the fifties and seventies. Missing, however, was this meticulous investigation by Ilán Stavans, which catalogues the tradition of the detective narrative, not so recent in origin nor as marginal as one might expect, now that its history has been traced to the forties, and the number of addicts and subscribers seems to place the genre among those most frequented by Mexican writers of late.

The unprepared reader may be surprised to find some of the major names in contemporary Mexican literature included in the detective genre. For one, Alfonso Reyes "stuck his neck out" for the detective novel at a very early point, by his own confession; the anthology of his complete works contains no fewer than three stories dedicated to the theme: "Algo más sobre la novela detectivesca," "Un gran policía de antaño," and the one to which I previously alluded, "Sobre la novela policial." One must also consider Rodolfo Usigli, Carlos Fuentes, Vicente Leñero, Jorge Ibargüengoitia, and José Emilio Pacheco among those who have contributed to the genre's enrichment.

The incorporation of Usigli, Fuentes, and Pacheco is questionable, since it is based on a single piece from each (Usigli's *Ensayo de un crimen,* Fuentes' *The Hydra Head,* Pacheco's *Morirás lejos*), and even thus, there is no consensus as to the strict detective character of these novels. North American critic Amelia S. Simpson considers Usigli's novel the first in Mexico's detective genre, and Stavans agrees with her, stating: "*Ensayo de un crimen* may be the finest novel written in Mexico." However, María Elvira Bermúdez, critic and author of a detective novel and various short stories herself, calls Usigli's work stupendous, but not "strictly a detective novel." Personally, I feel the same way about Fuentes's text, except that, judging it among his other works, I would not categorize it as outstanding either. Stavans vacillates between placing it in the espionage genre (which, in my judgment, is not the same as the detective genre), and considering it "a(n) homage to detective literature." But, in my opinion, Fuentes' novel fits very nicely into what, in the excellent critical portion of his work ("Parody and the Police"), Stavans himself defines as a "parodical stylization." Fuentes laughs openly at the tricks and maneuvers in espionage novels like the James Bond series, but without limiting the book's intrigue to suspense, the rationality of the events, much less the rigourous deductive logic which characterizes the traditional detective novel (from Poe to Conan Doyle and Simenon), and is also found in the North American thriller or hard-boiled novel (Dashiell Hammett, Raymond Chandler, Ross MacDonald, and so on).

As far as José Emilio Pacheco's admirable text, *Morirás lejos,* I must admit my reservations about categorizing it as what we conventionally consider detective literature; nonetheless, I must pay tribute to Ilán Stavans's critical wisdom for dedicating some of the more penetrating, lucid pages of his study to an analysis of this novel. Utilizing the theories of reception of Hans Robert Jauss (*Toward an Aesthetic of Reception*), Wolfgang Iser (*The Implied Reader, The Act of Reading*), and Umberto Eco (*Lector in Fabula*), Stavans proposes an interpretation through which Pacheco's piece is resolved as "a detective anti-novel where good does not triumph and one's intellect is diverted, exploring its own limits. More than a mere pastime, it is a map of the fallible and open universe of rationality." An ingenious formula, without a doubt, even when, according to my own reading, Pacheco's text escapes generic classification and is structured as an intertwined multiplicity of narrative voices within the fragmentation of time and space, aimed toward the recapitulation of one of the major dramas in western history. By the same magnitude of this drama, the characters, conflicts, situations, intrigue, and other elements which articulate the plot of a typical detective novel (or simply a *novel*) melt away and disappear, obliging the reader, unassisted, to grasp the text's naked, persuasive efficacy.

If, perhaps, the inclusion of these three major authors in a study on the Mexican detective novel provokes some resentment, it should not do so for the likes of Vicente Leñero and Jorge Ibargüengoitia. Both writers show a persistant inclination toward weaving the fictional plot of their narrations to support a theme with detective or criminal character. In Leñero's case, at least four novels maintain a clear affiliation with the genre: beginning with *Los albañiles*, followed by *Estudio Q, El garabato*, and *Asesinato. El doble crimen de los Flores Muñoz*, the latter a text to which Leñero himself refers as a "report or novel without fiction." As far as Ibargüengoitia is concerned, his work had already shown an unmistakable inclination toward the detective genre with his theatrical piece, *El atentado*, based on the assassination of General Alvaro Obregon, which won the Casa de las Americas prize in 1963; later he would reaffirm this same tendency in two or perhaps three of his novels: *Maten al león, The Dead Girls*, and *Two crimes;* the two-decade separation between first and last are indicative of Ibargüengoitia's firm commitment to the genre.

Once these clarifications have been made, one can unreservedly endorse the selection of writers through which Stavans elaborates his rigorous investigative history of the Mexican detective novel. This review is carried out in chapter 2, beginning with an analysis of Antonio Helú's initiatory work ("the cornerstone of detective letters in Mexico," and continues with Rodolfo Usigli, Rafael Solana, José Martinez de la Vega, María Elvira Bermúdez, Rafael Bernal, Carlos Fuentes, Sergio Pitol, and Rafael Ramírez Heredia. This inevitably uneven literary path, in terms of quality, volume, and importance, culminates, as one would expect, with a more thorough study of the contribution of Paco Ignacio Taibo II, unquestionably the most representative figure of the contemporary Mexican detective novel, and one of the few to establish a solid international reputation for the genre, his work published in countless editions and translations.

Of all authors, Paco Ignacio Taibo II has been the most successful in assimilating and transplanting to the Mexican scene (and, as Stavans accurately observes, principally to Mexico City, the Distrito Federal) the techniques, themes, style, and even language of the North American thriller, a form that in writers such as Dashiell Hammett, Raymond Chandler, and James Cain, among others, was known as "poetry" or "the aesthetic of violence." The tradition of the hard-boiled novel of the forties and fifties has inspired various international efforts, and its present validity can be seen in the works of numerous practitioners of the detective genre in the United States and Europe, as well as Latin America. Perhaps the most notorious cases (in Castillian, at least), along with Paco Ignacio Taibo II, are the Argentine Osvaldo Soriano (*Triste, solitario y final, A sus plantas rendido un león*) and the Spaniards Eduardo Mendoza (*The Truth about the Savolta Case,* Manuel Vázquez

Montalbán (*Tatuaje*), and, above all, Antonio Muñoz Molina (*El invierno en Lisboa, Beltenebros*).

Another contribution by Stavans's book (I am not sure if it is entirely original, one would have to compare it to other recent studies of Mexican literature), is to paint a historical, ideological, and cultural picture of Mexico under the PRI since the revolution's victory, following the events of Tlatelolco in 1968. The novel born there, particularly the nucleus of writers who are identified with the label of "La Onda," or "The Wave" (José Agustín, Gustavo Sainz, among others), breaks from the solemnity of a stultified literature and initiates changes which adjust the parameters of what has been called postmodernity, in particular the attempt to abolish the distinction between "serious" and "popular" culture; or as Stavans aptly writes, an art which "glorified counterculture, drugs, the opposition enraged by the establishment, and alternative understandings." That change in attitude appears to pave the way for the advent of the Mexican thriller, as it will be practiced by Paco Ignacio Taibo II and other authors of that generation, which permits the establishment of a certain synchronization between current detective fiction in Mexico and the socio-cultural changes that psychologists and critics identify with *postmodernity*.

The most original, significant contribution of Ilan Stavans's enchanting book-long essay isn't the fruition of his meticulous reading, investigation, compilation, and classification, but rather the establishment of the appropriate theoretical mark for analyzing the structural, linguistic, and narrative works upon which the detective novel is founded, deliberately or not, regardless of whether or not the author is aware. Stavans cites theoretical categories from Bakhtin's studies, so frequently recognized, utilized, and transplanted with diverse critical purposes, but perhaps never so well applied as in Stavans's specific analysis of detective literature. The essay also covers the already classic studies of the genre (Tzvetan Todorov, Roger Caillois, Dennis Porter, and so on), but it is in the concepts of parody, social hybrid, generic memory, stylization, parodical stylization, and variation, elaborated by Bakhtin in *The Dialogic Imagination* and *Problems of Dostoevsky's Poetics*, where Stavans finds the theoretical model to convincingly explain the structural, semantic, and even ideological strategies of this genre.

While articulating this theoretical discourse in the book's first section ("Parody and the Police"), Stavans goes much farther than propose the interpretive keys of the detective novel: he manages to connect the detective narrative as it has been practiced in Mexico with the rest of Latin American narrative, placing it among this narrative flow as a possible variation of the predominant themes, content, and tendencies. He seems to suggest, furthermore, that detective literature is not distinct nor is it essentially unlike the parodical vocation that Latin American literary-cultural discourse has maintained since its colonial origens (*The Itching Parrot, El lazarillo de ciegos caminantes*, "The Slaughterhouse"). It is worth remembering here, as Stavans himself does in this volume, that many of the major writers of Latin American literature recurrently practiced the genre, beginning with Jorge Luis Borges and Adolfo Bioy Casares, up through the so-called boom generation, and more recently, the aforementioned Carlos Fuentes, Mario Vergas Llosa (*Who Killed Palomino Molero?*), Gabriel García Márquez (*Chronicle of a Death Foretold*), Manuel Puig (*The Buenos Aires Affair*), and so on. If the intention of these texts is to "parodize," with an unmistakably Latin American accent, a genre whose roots are in Europe and the United States, Stavans's assertion is fully justified when he writes: "This cultural adaptation is, in reality, the leitmotif of Ibero-American art. The dichotomy of the foreign models and the loyalty to idols or native idiosyncracy is ever-present in the veins of the intelligentsia even now. Thus, the idea of parody is well entrenched in this culture, not always via humor but through variation, stylization, appropriation, and, above all, by way of generic memory, to which the writers of Mexico City, Río de la Plata, Lima or Bogotá come to feed themselves."

HIBER CONTERIS

Notes

Introduction

1. Dennis Porter, *The Pursuit of Crime* (New Haven and London: Yale University Press, 1981), p. 1.

2. A book which is a collection of principal critical tendencies, of great use to anyone interested, is *The Poetics of Murder: Detective Fiction and Literary Theory* (New York: Harcourt Brace Jovanovich, 1983), Glenn W. Most and William W. Stowe, eds. See page XI for a summary.

3. Patricia Hart, *The Spanish Sleuth* (Madison and Teaneck: Fairleigh Dickinson University Press, 1987).

Chapter 1. Point of Departure

1. Octavio Paz, *Posdata* (Mexico: Siglo XXI Editores, 1970, 13th ed., 1979), 40.

2. There are many studies which are useful in the study of the complete panorama of twentieth-century Mexican literature: Joseph Sommers, *After the Storm. Landmarks of the Modern Mexican Novel* (Albuquerque: University of New Mexico Press, 1968); Walter M. Langford, *The Mexican Novel Comes of Age* (Notre Dame and London: University of Notre Dame Press, 1971); Emanuel Carballo, *Diecinueve protagonistas de la literatura mexicana del siglo XX* (Mexico: Empresas Editoriales, 1965); Jorge Rufinelli, "Notas sobre la novela mexicana, 1975–1980," *Cuadernos de Marcha* (July-August 1981): 47–59; and Margo Glantz, *Repeticiones: Ensayos sobre literatura mexicana* (Jalapa: Universidad Veracruzana, 1979).

3. Carlos de Sigüenza y Góngora, *Alboroto y motín de México del 8 de junio de 1692* (Talleres Gráficos del Museo Nacional de Antropología, Historia y Etnografía, 1932); Sor Juana Inés de la Cruz, *Neptuno alegórico* (vol. 4, *Obras Completas*, Fondo de Cultura Económica, 1951).

4. Arturo Azuela, *Manifestación de silencios* (Mexico: Joaquín Mortiz, 1979); Luis Spota, *Paraíso 25* (Mexico: Grijalbo, 1982); José Emilio Pacheco, *Las batallas en el desierto* (Mexico: Era, 1981); Luis Zapata, *El vampiro de la Colonia Roma* (Mexico: Grijalbo, 1979); and "El prisionero de Las Lomas," a short novel in *Constancia* (Mexico: Fondo de Cultura Económica, 1990) and *Cristóbal Nonato* (Mexico: Fondo de Cultura Económica, 1987), both from Carlos Fuentes. At an academic and investigative level, many historical studies have sprung up about the Distrito Federal. For example: Fernando Benítez and *La ciudad de México, 1325–1982* (3 vols. Mexico: Fondo de Cultura Económica, 1977–78); also, in English, Jonathan Kandell's *La Capital: The Biography of Mexico City* (New York: Random House, 1988).

5. John S. Brushwood, *La novela mexicana (1967–1982)* (Mexico: Grijalbo,

Colección Enlace, 1985), 17. In addition, its precursor volume, *Mexico in Its Novel. A Nation's Search for Identity* (Austin: University of Texas Press, 1966). The Mexican translation from the Fondo de Cultura Económica is from 1973.

Chapter 2. Parody and the Police

1. Alex Preminger, *Princeton Encyclopedia of Poetry and Poetics*, (New Jersey: Princeton University Press, 1965, 1974), 600–2. Some other valuable recent works that discuss this theme are Michele Hannoosh, "The Reflexive Function of Parody," *Comparative Literature* 41, no. 2 (Spring 1989): 113–27; Robin Howells, "Burlesque and Parody," *French Studies Bulletin: A Quarterly Supplement* 31 (1989): 13–19; Jean Jacques Hamm, "Parodie: Theorie et lecture," *Etudes Litteraires* 19, no. 1 (1986): 12–19; and Maja Herman-Sekulic, "Toward a New Understanding of Parody," *European Studies Journal* 2, no. 2 (1985): 7–13.

2. M. M. Bakhtin, *The Dialogic Imagination,* ed. Michael Holquist, trans. Caryl Emerson and Michael Holquist (Austin: University of Texas Press, 1981), 41–83.

3. Ibid., 165.

4. Maurice Keen, *Chivalry* (New Haven and London: Yale University Press, 1984), 239.

5. M. M. Bakhtin, *Problems of Dostoevsky's Poetics,* trans. R. W. Rotsel (Ann Arbor, Mich.: Ardis, 1973).

6. Bakhin, *The Dialogic Imagination,* 259–422.

7. Emir Rodríguez Monegal, "Carnaval/Antropofagia/Parodia," *Revista Iberamericana,* no. 108–9 (July-December 1979): 401–12.

8. Ibid., 407.

9. Hernán Vidal, *Literatura hispanoamericana e ideología liberal: surgimiento y crisis (una problemática sobre la dependencia en torno a la narrativa del Boom)* (Buenos Aires: Hispamérica, 1988). Precursors of this argument are Borges in *Indice* (1926) and Alejo Carpentier in the prologue to *El reino de este mundo* (1979).

10. See my "Cervantes para Borges," *Anthropos,* no. 98–99 (1989): IX.

11. John Barth, "Literature of Exhaustion," *The Atlantic Monthly* 220, no. 2 (August 1967). The quote comes from the Spanish translation of Jorge Luis Borges. Edition of Jaime Alazraki (Madrid: Taurus, 1976), 175.

12. In this sense Emir Rodríguez Monegal's introductions in *Borzoi Anthology of Latin American Literature,* 2 vols. (New York: Alfred A. Knopf, 1976) are revealing.

13. Carlos Fuentes, *Myself with Others* (New York: Farrar, Straus & Giroux, 1988), 31.

14. Monegal, ed., *Borzoi Anthology,* 2:14.

Chapter 3. ABC, or the Formula

1. Porter, *Pursuit of Crime,* 30–1.

2. Boris Tomashevsky, "Thematics," in *Russian Formalist Criticism: Four Essays,* ed. by Lee T. Lemon and Marion J. Reis (University Nebraska Press, 1965), 68.

3. Ibid., 82.

4. Arthur Conan Doyle, *Complete Works* (London: Penguin, 1984), 21.

5. Roger Caillois, "The Detective Novel as Game," in *The Poetics of Murder*, 12.

Chapter 4. Brief Overview

1. *Roots of Detection. The Art of Deduction Before Sherlock Holmes*, ed. by Bruce Cassiday (New York: Ungar, 1983), 1.
2. Julian Symons, *Bloody Murder. From the Detective Story to the Crime Novel* (London: Penguin, 1985), 130.
3. For a study of James Bond, see Umberto Eco, "Narrative Structures in Fleming," *The Poetics of Murder*, 93–117.

Chapter 5. Constables and Sentries

1. Ernest, Mandel, *Delightful Murder: A Social History of the Crime Story* (Minneapolis: University of Minnesota Press, 1984), 16.
2. See Walter Benjamin, "Kriminalromane auf Reisen" in, *Gesammelte Schriften*, vol. 10 (Frankfurt am-Main: Werkausgabe, 1975), 381–2.
3. Mark A. Burkholder, and Lyman L. Johnson, *Colonial Latin America* (New York: Oxford University Press, 1990).
4. Ibid., 15.
5. Arturo Sotomayor, "Del sereno al académico," in "Ficción y Realidad: Detectives," *Comunidad Conacyt*, special issue on detective fiction edited by Enrique Loubet, Jr. (III, noms. 121–122, January–February 1981), 164.
6. Ibid., 150.
7. It is worthwhile to emphasize that in Mexican detective letters the appearance of these words refers to members of the police force; usage always depends upon the historical context, the situation, and the intention of the writer.
8. Edgardo Montiel Govea. "Datos históricos del uniforme de la Policía Preventiva," *Comunidad Conacyt*, 161–64.
9. Ibid., 163.
10. Octavio Paz, *The Labyrinth of Solitude* (New York: Grove Press, Inc., 1961), 70.

Chapter 6. Real-Life Cases

1. *Encyclopedia of Mystery and Detection*, ed. by Chris Steinbrunner and Otto Penzler (San Diego, London, and New York: Harcourt, Brace and Jovanovich, 1984).
2. Carlos Borbolla, "Los detectives en la vida real," *Comunidad Conacyt*, 138–42.
3. Jean Meyer, *Los Cristeros* (Mexico: El Colegio de México, 1977).
4. Monsiváis, Carlos. *Amor perdido* (Mexico: Biblioteca Era, 1977), 114–5. In the end, Siqueiros managed to escape from Lecumberri and appeared several months later in Santiago, Chile.
5. *Comunidad Conacyt*, 119–32.
6. See the last volume of the trilogy by Isaac Deutscher, *The Prophet Outcast: 1929–1940* (Cambridge: Oxford University Press, 1963).
7. The discoveries of Dr. Alfonso Quiróz Cuarón were published in 1957 in a magazine out of Sorbonne, *Etudes Internationales de Psycho-Sociologie Crimi-*

nelle de Paris. In 1980, José Ramón Garmabella published a book at Editorial Diana called *Dr. Alfonso Quiroz Cuarón: Sus mejores casos de criminología.*

Chapter 7. The Critic's Voice

1. Luis Leal, *Historia del cuento hispanoamericano* (Mexico: Ediciones de Andrea, 1971), 142.
2. Sábato, Ernesto. *Heterodoxia,* 1953 (Barcelona: Seix-Barral, 1982), 47.
3. "Algo más sobre la novela detectivesca" and "Un gran policía de antaño," vol. 21, "Marginalia," *Obras Completas of Alfonso Reyes* (Fondo de Cultura Económica, 1989), 412–20; and "Sobre la novela policial," vol. 9, "Los trabajos y los días" (Fondo de Cultura Económica, 1959), 457–61.
4. Paco Ignacio Taibo II, "La (otra) novela policiaca," *Los Cuadernos del Norte,* 7, no. 41 (March-April 1987): 40.
5. Carlos Monsiváis, "Ustedes que jamás han sido asesinados," *Revista de la Universidad de México,* vol. 28, no. 7 (March 1973), 11.
6. *Los mejores cuentos policiacos mexicanos,* ed. María Elvira Bermúdez (Mexico: Biblioteca Mínima, 1955).
7. Vicente Francisco Torres, "La literatura policiaca mexicana," *Comunidad Conacyt,* 81.
8. Anthony Boucher, "It's Murder, Amigos: The Mystery Story Takes Root in Latin America," *Publishers Weekly* 19 (April 1947).
9. Among them "The Spanish American Detective Story," *Modern Language Journal* (May 1956); and "La novela policial en las Américas" *Temas culturales* (1963). But his most important article on the subject for our purposes is "The Mexican Detective Story," *Kentucky Foreign Language Review,* 3, no. 1 (1961): 42–47.
10. *El cuento policial latinamericano,* introduction, selection, and biography by Donald A. Yates (Mexico: Ediciones de Andrea, 1964). Also by Yates is *Latin Blood: The Best Crime and Detective Stories of South America* (New York: Herder & Herder, 1972.)
11. Yates, *El cuento policial latinamericano,* 4.
12. *El cuento policial mexicano,* prologue and selection by V. F. Torres (Mexico: Editorial Diógenes, S.A., 1982), 13–4.
13. Antonio Panells in Escritura, "El detective literario: Panorámica del género policiaco de Poe a Borges," no. 10, 19–20 (1985): 41–101. A section was reprinted as "El género policiaco en Hispanoamérica," in a special edition of *Monographic Review/Revista Monográfica,* "Hispanic Science-Fiction/Fantasy and The Thriller" 3, no. 1–2 (1987): 148–62.
14. Eugenia Revueltas, "La novela policial en México y en Cuba," *Cuadernos Americanos,* Nueva Epoca, 1, no. 1 (January-February 1987): 102–20.
15. Amelia S. Simpson, *Detective Fiction from Latin America* (Madison and Teaneck: Fairleigh Dickinson University Press, 1990), 96.

Chapter 8. Antonio Helú

1. *El cuento enigmático,* selection, notes and prologue by Antonio Helú (Mexico: Secretaría de Educación Pública, 1968).
2. According to Donald A. Yates, an anagram of the Spanish word *ladrón,* or thief. *El cuento policial latinoamericano,* 12.
3. Simpson, *Detective Fiction,* 88.

4. See the autobiography of Juan Bustillo Oro published in *México en la Cultura,* part of which appeared in book form under the title *México de mi infancia* no. 43 (Mexico: Colección Metropolitana, 1975).

5. Torres, *El cuento,* 82.

6. Ibid., 13.

7. Ibid., 27.

8. Ibid., 178.

Chapter 9. Rodolfo Usigli

1. Simpson, *Detective Fiction,* 87.

2. *Comunidad Conacyt,* 84.

3. *Comunidad Conacyt,* 84.

4. Rodolfo Usigli, *Ensayo de un crimen* (Mexico: Aguilar León y Cal Editores, 1989), 212–13.

5. José De la Colina, and Tomás Pérez Turrent, *Luis Buñuel: Prohibido asomarse al interior* (Mexico: Joaquín Mortiz/Planeta, 1986), 105–12.

Chapter 10. Rafael Solana

1. His bibliography includes the novel *El envenenado* (illustrations and vignettes by Juan Soriano [Mexico: Taller, 1939]); the work *Debiera haber obispas* (Mexico: Editores Mexicanos Unidos, 1985); and a collection of stories, the title of which is identical to one by Spanish writer Miguel Delibes, *Los santos inocentes* (Mexico: Géminis, 1949).

2. *El cuento policial mexicano,* 16.

3. Solana, Rafael, *El crimen de tres bandas* (Mexico: Colección Lunes, 1945), 27.

Chapter 11. José Martínez de la Vega

1. Two examples are *Heriberto Jara; un hombre de la Revolución* (Mexico: Editorial Diálogo, 1964); and *30 disparates sin prólogo . . . (Un libro de buen humor)* (Mexico: Talleres Gráficos de Excélsior, 1944).

2. José Martínez de la Vega, *Péter Pérez, detective de Peralvillo y anexas* (Mexico, n.d., 1952), 9.

3. Torres, *Comunidad Conacyt,* 84. In her 1955 anthology, Bermúdez includes the story "El misterio de la lata de sardinas," as does Torres in his 1982 collection.

4. Donald A. Yates, *El cuento policial latinoamericano,* 9.

5. Ibid., 89–96.

6. "Ensayo para el sainete mexicano," *Péter Pérez, detective de Peralvillo y anexas,* 153–55. The parts were filled by Guillermo Portillo Acosta as Péter Pérez, Salvador Carrasco as Juan Vélez, as well as Luis Vadillo, Carlota Solares, don Ernesto Finance, Luis Pelayo, and Rosario Muñoz Ledo.

Chapter 12. María Elvira Bermúdez

1. María Elvira Bermúdez, *Detente, sombra* (Mexico: Universidad Autónoma Metropolitana). In addition, she has written studies of the Mexican personality along the lines of those by Santiago Ramírez and Samuel Ramos.

2. Refer especially to "En defensa de la novela policiaca," *El Nacional* (24 September 1978), 8.

3. *Tales of the Grotesque and Arabesque* by Edgar Allan Poe, in prologue by María Elvira Bermúdez (Mexico: Series "Sepan cuántos . . . ," Editorial Porrúa, 1972); *Capitán Tormenta* by Emilio Salgari, in prologue by María Elvira Bermúdez; (México: Series "Sepan cuántos . . ." Editorial Porrúa, 1982); *Miguel Strogoff* by Jules Verne, in prologue by María Elvira Bermúdez (Mexico: Series "Sepan cuántos . . ." Editorial Porrúa, 1971).

4. In addition to the authors already mentioned, she included Rubén Salazar Mallén, Daniel Cosío Villegas, and the pseudonym of an unknown author: Leo D'Olmo.

5. *Diferentes razones tiene la muerte* (Mexico, n.d.); *Muerte a la zaga* (Mexico: Premiá/Secretaría de Educación Pública, 1986).

6. Bermúdez, *Diferentes razones tiene la muerte*, 118.

7. *El cuento policial mexicano*, 16.

8. *Comunidad Conacyt*, 85.

9. Taibo II, "La (otra) novela policiaca," 36–41.

10. See Jean Franco, *Plotting Women. Gender & Representation in Mexico* (New York: Columbia University Press, 1989).

Chapter 13. Rafael Bernal

1. "La (otra) novela policiaca," 38.

2. Rafael Bernal, *Tierra de gracia* (Mexico, 1936).

3. Rafael Bernal, *En diferentes mundos* (Mexico: Fondo de Cultura Económica, 1967).

4. Rafael Bernal, *El complot mongol* (Mexico: Joaquín Mortiz, 1989), 9–10.

5. Ibid., 26.

6. Rafael Bernal, *Un muerto en la tumba* (Mexico: Editorial Jus, 1988), 141.

7. *Antología de cuentos mexicanos*, ed. by María del Carmen Millán, 1976 (2 vols., 9th ed. Mexico: Editorial Nueva Imagen, 1990). "La media hora de Sebastián Constantino" is included in 1: 161–71; "La Décima," by Rafael Solana, also appears, 95–105.

Chapter 14. Carlos Fuentes

1. Jaime Alazraki, "Theme and System in Carlos Fuentes' *Aura*," *Carlos Fuentes: A Critical View*, ed. Robert Brody and Charles Rossman (Austin, Texas: University of Texas Press, 1982), 95–105.

2. Carlos Fuentes, *The Hydra Head* (New York: Farrar, Straus, Giroux, 1978). Amelia S. Simpson says that "it is a tribute to film noir and the tradition of the thriller," 94.

3. The text is full of references to paintings and mirrors. See Mary E. Davis, "On Becoming Velázquez: Carlos Fuentes' *The Hydra Head*." *Carlos Fuentes: A Critical View*, 146–55.

4. Ilan Stavans, "Perfil del judío en *La cabeza de la hidra* de Carlos Fuentes," *La historia de la literatura iberoamericana*. Essays from the XXXVI Congreso del Instituto Internacional de Literatura Iberoamericana. Edited, compiled and prologued by Raquel Chang-Rodríguez and Graciella de Beer (New Hampshire: Ediciones del Norte, 1989), 235–42.

5. Fuentes, *The Hydra Head*, 38.
6. Ibid., 41.

Chapter 15. Sergio Pitol, Rafael Ramírez Heredia, et al.

1. *The New York Times*, Sunday 30 August 1988, "Arts and Leisure," 32.
2. In *Crímenes ejemplares*, Torres claims that Aub "searched for the disconcerting but human quality in the delinquents' declarations" (*El cuento policial mexicano*, 15). Because of his large estate in Mexico, Torres considers Aub Mexican, though he was never naturalized.
3. Sergio Pitol, *El desfile del amor* (Barcelona: Editorial Anagrama, 1984).
4. Rafael Ramírez Heredia, *La jaula de Dios* (Mexico: Joaquín Mortiz, 1989).
5. Rafael Ramírez Heredia, *Trampa de metal* (Mexico: Editorial Joaquín Mortiz, 1993; 1st ed. Editorial Universo, 1979).
6. Rafael Ramírez Heredia, *Muerte en la carretera* (Mexico: Joaquín Mortiz, 1985).
7. Ibid., 27.

Chapter 16. Paco Ignacio Taibo II

1. G. Cabrera Infante, *El País* (Madrid, 11 January 1987): 25.
2. P. I. Taibo II, *Cosa fácil*, 1987 (Mexico: Planeta, 1989).
3. Paco Ignacio Taibo I, *Siempre Dolores* (Mexico: Joaquín Mortiz, 1993); *De algún tiempo a esta parte* (2 vols. Mexico: Alianza Editorial Mexicana, 1990).
4. P. I. Taibo II, *La batalla del Ché: Santa Clara* (Mexico: Planeta, 1988).
5. *Bajando la frontera: Jack London, John Reed, John K. Turner, Richard F. Phillips, Mike Gold, Lynn A. E. Gale, Brertrom D. Wolfe, Carleton Beals*. Prologue, selection, and notes by P. I. Taibo II (Mexico: Crónica General de México/ Leega Jucar, 1985).
6. José C. Valadés, *El socialism libertario mexicano. Siglo XIX*. Prologue and compilation by P. I. Taibo II (Mexico: Universidad Autónoma de Sinaloa, 1984).
7. *Días de combate* (Mexico: Planeta, 1976); *Cosa fácil; No habrá final feliz* (Mexico: Planeta, 1989); *Algunas nubes* (Mexico: Leega, 1985); *Sombra de la sombra* (Mexico: Planeta, 1986); *La vida misma* (Mexico: Leega, 1987); and *Regreso a la misma ciudad y bajo la lluvia* (Mexico: Planeta, 1989). The first two have been adapted to film, under the direction of Alfredo Gurrola and acted by Pedro Armendáriz, Jr.
8. Taibo II, *Regreso a la misma*, 17.
9. Raymond Chandler, "Causal Notes on the Mystery Novel," *Raymond Chandler Speaking*, ed. by Dorthy Gardiner and Katherine Sorley Walker (Boston: Houghton Mifflin, 1977).
10. *Arcángeles. Cuatro historias no muy ortodoxas de revolucionarios* (Mexico: Alianza Editorial Mexicana, 1988).
11. Taibo II, *No Happy Ending*, translated by William I. Neuman (New York: The Mysterious Press, 1993), 18.
12. John Dickson Carr, *The Life of Sir Arthur Conan Doyle* (New York: Harper & Row, 1949).
13. Taibo II, *No Happy Ending*, 174–5.
14. Taibo II, *Regreso a la misma*, 9.

15. Torres, *El cuento policial mexicano,* 83.

Chapter 17. Revolutionizing the Formula

1. Dennis Porter, *The Pursuit of Crime. Art and Ideology in Detective Fiction* (New Haven and London: Yale University Press, 1981), 256.

Chapter 18. Vicente Leñero

1. Vicente Leñero, *Estudio Q* (Mexico: Joaquín Mortiz, 1965), 300.
2. A similar game of mirrors occurs in *Miscast,* the theatrical work by Salvador Elizondo (Mexico: Editorial Oasis, 1981), written to order for the Instituto Nacional de Bellas Artes and the Secretaría de Educación Pública, where the identity of the authors is confused with that of its characters.
3. It is Luciana Figueroa's thesis in "Los códigos de veridicción en *El garabato,* de Vicente Leñero," *Simiosis* no. 4 (1980): 31–59.
4. Vicente Leñero's *Los albañiles* (Mexico: Planeta/Seix Barral, 1974). Among others, Mario Vargas Llosa won the same prize for *La ciudad y los perros* (*The time of the hero*).
5. Vicente Leñero, *Asesinato. El doble crimen de los Flores Muñoz* (Mexico: Plaza & Janes, 1985).
6. *Los albañile*s, 249–50.
7. See Humberto E. Robles, "Aproximación a *Los albañiles* de Vicente Leñero," *Revista Iberoamericana* 73 (1970), 579–99. For a panoramic vision of the author's work, see *Vicente Leñero. The Novelist as Critic.* by Danny J. Anderson, part of the University of Texas Studies of Contemporary Spanish-American Fiction (New York-Frankfurt am Main: Peter Lang, 1989).
8. Amelia S. Simpson, *Detective Fiction from Latin America,* 146–52.
9. Iris Josefina Ludmer, "Vicente Leñero, *Los albañiles.* Lector y actor," *Nueva novela latinoamericana,* Jorge Laforgue, ed. (Buenos Aires: Paidós, 1969).
10. Tzvetan Todorov, *The Poetics of Prose* (New York: Cornell University Press, 1977).
11. "*Los albañiles* de Vicente Leñero, dentro de las novelas de detectives" by Ricardo Szmetan, *Confluencia* 4, no. 2 (Spring 1989): 67–71.
12. *Los albañiles,* theatrical adaptation by Vicente Leñero (Mexico: Joaquín Mortiz, 1970).
13. Vicente Leñero, *Vivir del teatro* (Mexico: Joaquín Mortiz, 1982), 12.
14. Ibid., 5.

Chapter 19. Jorge Ibarüengoitia

1. Jorge Ibargüengoitia, "Otras voces, otras teatros. La vida en México en tiempos de Novo," *Excélsior* (18 February 1974).
2. "Jorge Ibargüengoitia dice de sí mismo," *Vuelta,* no. 100 (March 1985).
3. Ibargüengoitia, *Las muertas* (Mexico: Joaquín Mortiz, 1977; rev. 1989).
4. Ibargüengoitia, *Dos crímenes* (Mexico: Joaquín Mortiz, 1979; rev. 1992).
5. See "Ambigüedad de la novela," *El arco y la lira* by Octavio Paz (Mexico: Joaquín Mortiz, 1956), 219–31.
6. Octavio Paz, *México en la obra de Octavio Paz,* vol. 2, "Generaciones y semblanzas. Escritores y letras en México." O. Paz and L. Mario Schneider, eds. (Mexico: Fondo de Cultura Económica, 1987), 587–88.

7. Ibid., 7.

8. Eduardo Mendoza, *La verdad sobre el caso Savolta*, (Barcelona: Seix-Barral, 1975).

9. Jorge Ibargüengoitia, *Autopsias rápidas*. Selected by Guillermo Sheridan (Mexico: Vuelta, Colección La Reflexión, 1988), 76–77.

10. This novel by Ibargüengoitia, along with *El Señor Presidente* by Miguel Angel Asturias, *El recurso del método* (Reasons of state) by Alejo Carpentier, *Yo el Supremo* (I the Supreme) by Augusto Roa Bastos, *Conversación en La Catedral* (Conversation in the catedral) by Mario Vargas Llosa, and *El otoño del patriarca* (Autumn of the patriarch) by Gabriel García Márquez, can be filed under the category of "dictator's novel."

11. Ibargüengoitia, "Homage to James Bond," *The Literary Review*, 38 no. 1 (Fall 1994): 98–99.

12. Ibargüengoitia, "Agatha Christie: An Unlikely Obituary," 45–46.

13. Ibargüengoitia, "Homage to James Bond," 98.

14. Ibargüengoitia, "Agatha Christie: An Unlikely Obituary," 45.

15. Jorge Ibargüengoitia, "En primera persona: Punto final," *Vuelta* no. 31 (June 1979).

16. For example, Jaime Castañeda Iturbide's *El humorismo desmitificador de Jorge Ibargüengoitia* (Mexico: Gobierno del Estado de Guanajuato, 1988), 85–93.

17. Jorge Ibargüengoitia, "¿De qué viven los escritores?" *Revista de la Universidad de México*, 17 no. 4, December 1962.

18. Ibid., 129.

Chapter 20. José Emilio Pacheco

1. José Emilio Pacheco, *Morirás lejos* (Mexico: Joaquín Mortiz, 1967; rev., 1977). In addition, there is a Spanish edition (Montesinos, 1980). The 1977 version is cited here.

2. Ibid., 45.

3. Boris Tomashevsky, "Thematics," *Russian Formalist Criticism: Four Essays* translated and with an introduction by Lee T. Leman and Marion J. Reis (Lincoln: University of Nebraska Press, 1965), 68–72.

4. Ibid., 82.

5. Ibid., 6.

6. Ibid., 6.

7. Wolfgang Iser, *The Implied Reader: Patterns of Communication in Prose Fiction from Bunyan to Beckett* (Baltimore: Johns Hopkins University Press, 1974); and *The Act of Reading: A Theory of Aesthetic Response* (Baltimore: Johns Hopkins University Press, 1979).

8. Pacheco, *Morirás lejos,*: (a) 6, (b) 12, (c) 15, (d) 17, (e) 21, (f) 22, (g) 24, (h) 27, (i) 29, (j) 30, (k) 30, (l) 31, (m) 33, (n) 35, (ñ) 36, (o) 37, (p) 38, (q) 39, (r) 42, (s) 45, (t) 47, (u) 50, (v) 58, (y) 65, (z) 65.

9. Ibid., 66.

10. Umberto Eco, *Lector in fabula;* in English as *The Role of the Reader* (Bloomington and London: Indiana University Press, 1979).

11. Hans Robert Jauss, *Aesthetic Experience and Literary Hermeneutics,* translated by Michael Shaw, introduction by Wlad Godzing (Minneapolis: University of Minnesota Press, 1982).

12. Ibid., 5, the emphasis is mine.

13. Ibid., 6.

14. Ibid., 125–6.

15. Ibid., 8–9.

Bibliography

Alazraki, Jaime. "Theme and System in Carlos Fuentes' *Aura*," *Carlos Fuentes: A Critical View*. Robert Brody and Charles Rossman, eds. Austin: University of Texas Press, 1982.

Anderson, Danny J. *Vicente Leñero: The Novelist as Critic*. University of Texas Press, Studies of Contemporary Spanish-American Fiction. New York and Frankfurt-am-Main: Peter Lang, 1989.

Azuela, Arturo. *Manifestación de silencios*. Mexico: Joaquín Mortiz, 1979.

Bajarlía, Juan Jacobo, ed. *Cuentos de crimen y de misterio*. Buenos Aires: José Alvarez, 1964.

Bakhtin, Mikhail Mikhailovich. *The Dialogic Imagination: Four Essays*. Michael Holquist, ed. Translated by Carlyn Emerson and Michael Holquist. Austin: University of Texas Press, 1981.

———. *Problems of Dostoevsky's Poetics*. Translated by R. W. Rotsel. Ann Arbor, Michigan: Ardis, 1973.

Barth, John. "Literature of Exhaustion," *The Atlantic Monthly*, 220, no. 2 (August 1967).

Benítez, Fernando. *La Ciudad de México, 1325–1982*. 3 vols. Mexico: Fondo de Cultura Económica, 1977–78.

Benjamin, Walter. *Gesammelte Schriften*. Frankfurt-am-Main: Werkausgabe, 1975.

Bermúdez, María Elvira. *Muerte a la zaga*. Mexico: Premiá, 1986.

———. *Detente, sombra*. Mexico: Universidad Autónoma Metropolitana, 1984.

———. *Los mejores cuentos policiales mexicanos*. Mexico: Biblioteca Mínima, 1955.

———. *Diferentes razones tiene la muerte*. Mexico: n., 1947.

Bernal, Rafael. *El complot mongol*. Mexico: Joaquín Mortiz, 1989.

———. *En diferentes mundos*. Mexico: Fondo de Cultura Económica, 1967.

———. *Un muerto en la tumba*. Mexico: Jus, 1946.

Borges, Jorge Luis. *Seis problemas para don Isidro Parodi* (1942) and *Crónicas de Bustos Domecq* (1967), *Obras completas en colaboración*. Vol. 1 "Con Adolfo Bioy Casares." Madrid and Buenos Aires: Alianza Tres, Emecé Editores, 1981.

———. *Obras completas*. Buenos Aires: Emecé Editores, 1974.

Boucher, Anthony. "It's Murder, Amigos: The Mystery Story Takes Root in Latin America," *Publisher's Weekly*, 19 April 1947: 13–15.

Brushwood, John S. *La novela mexicana (1967–1982)*. Mexico: Grijalbo, 1985.

———. *Mexico in Its Novel: A Nations's Search for Identity*. Austin: University of Texas Press, 1966.

Burkholder, Mark A., with Lyman L. Johnson. *Colonial Latin America*. New York: Oxford University Press, 1990.

Bustillo Oro, Juan. *México de mi infancia*. Mexico: no. 43, Colección Metropolitana, 1975.

Cabrera Infante, Guillermo. "Holmes Sweet Holmes," *El País*, Madrid (11 January 1987): 25.

Caillois, Roger. *Le Roman Policier*. Buenos Aires: Sur, 1941.

Carballo, Emmanuel. *Diecinueve protagonistas de la literatura mexicana del siglo XX*. Mexico: Empresas Editoriales, 1965.

Carr, John Dickson. *The Life of Sir Arthur Conan Doyle*. New York:. Harper & Row, 1949.

Cassiday, Bruce, ed. *Roots of Detection: The Art of Deduction before Sherlock Holmes*. New York: Frederick Ungar, 1983.

Castañeda Iturbide, Jaime. *El humorismo desmitificador de Jorge Ibargüengoitia*. Mexico: Gobierno del Estado de Guanajuato, 1988.

Chandler, Raymond. "The Simple Art of Murder," in *The Simple Art of Murder*. New York: Ballantine, 1977: 1–21.

―――. "Casual Notes on the Mystery Novel," *Raymond Chandler Speaking*. Dorothy Gardiner and Katherine Sorley Walker, eds. Boston: Houghton Mifflin, 1977.

Colina, José de la, with Tomás Pérez Turrent. *Luis Buñuel: Prohibido asomarse al interior*. Mexico: Joaquín Mortiz-Planeta, 1986.

Conan Doyle, Arthur. *Complete Works*. Londres: Penguin, 1984.

Davis, Mary. "On Becoming Velázquez: Carlos Fuentes' *The Hydra Head*," *Carlos Fuentes: A Critical View*. Robert Brody and Charles Rossman, eds. Austin: University of Texas Press, 1982.

Deutscher, Isaac. *The Prophet Outcast: 1929–1940*. Cambridge: Oxford University Press, 1963.

Elizondo, Salvador. *Miscast*. Mexico: Editorial Oásis, 1981.

Eco, Umberto. *Lector in fabula: La cooperazione interpretative nei testi narrativi*. Milan: Bompiani, 1979.

Figueroa, Luciana. "Los códigos de verificación en *El garabato*, de Vicente Leñero," *Semiosis*, no. 4 (1980): 31–59

Franco, Jean. *Plotting Women. Gender & Representation in Mexico*. New York: Columbia University Press, 1989.

Frye, Northrop. *The Secular Scripture. A Study of Romance*. Cambridge: Harvard University Press, 1976.

―――. *Anatomy of Criticism: Four Essays*. Princeton: Princeton University Press, 1957.

Fuentes, Carlos. *Constancia y otras novelas para vírgenes*. Mexico: Fondo de Cultura Económica. 1990. *Constancia and Other Stories for Virgins*. Translated into English by Thomas Christensen. New York: Farrar, Straus & Giroux, 1990.

―――. "How I Wrote One of My Books," *Myself With Others*. New York: Farrar, Straus & Giroux. 1988: 28–45.

―――. *Cristóbal Nonato*. Mexico: Fondo de Cultura Económica, 1987. *Christopher Unborn*. Translated into English by Alfred Mac Adam. New York: Farrar, Straus & Giroux, 1989.

―――. *Aura*. Mexico: Era, 1978.

―――. *La cabeza de la hidra*. Mexico: Joaquín Mortiz, 1978. *The Hydra Head*.

Translated into English by Margaret Sayers Peden. New York: Farrar, Straus & Giroux, 1978.

————. *La región más transparente.* Mexico: Fondo de Cultura Económica, 1958. Translated into English by Sam Hileman under the title *Where the Air Is Clear.* New York: Farrar, Straus & Giroux, 1960.

Gardinelli, Mempo. *El género negro.* 2 vols. Mexico: Universidad Autónoma Metropolitana, 1984

Garmabella, José Ramón. *Dr. Alfonso Quiroz Cuaron: Sus mejores casos de criminología.* Mexico: Editorial Diana, 1980.

Glantz, Margo. *Repeticiones: Ensayos sobre la literatura mexicana.* Jalapa: Universidad Veracruzana, 1979.

Gual, Enrique F. *Asesinato en la plaza.* Mexico: Editorial Albatros, 1946.

————. *El caso de los Leventheris.* Mexico: Editorial Albatros, 1946.

————. *El crimen de la obsidiana.* Mexico: Ediciones Minerva, 1942.

Hamm, Jean-Jacques. "Parodie: Theorie et lecture," *Etudes Litteraires,* 19, no. 1 (Spring-Summer 1986): 12–19.

Hannoosh, Michele. "The Reflexive Function of Parody," *Comparative Literature,* 4, no. 2 (1989): 113–27.

Hart, Patricia. *The Spanish Sleuth. The Detective in Spanish Fiction.* Cranbury, New Jersey: Fairleigh Dickinson University Press, 1987.

Helú, Antonio, ed. *El cuento enigmático.* Mexico: Secretaría de Educación Pública, 1968.

————. *La obligación de asesinar.* Mexico: Albatros, 1947; 2 ed., with a prologue by Xavier Villaurrutia. Mexico: Editorial Novaro-México, S.A., 1957.

Hermann-Sekulic, Meja. "Toward a New Understanding of Parody," *European Studies Journal,* 2, no. 2 (1985): 7–13.

Howells, Robin. "Burlesque and Parody," *French Studies Bulletin: A Quarterly Supplement,* 31 (Summer 1989): 7–10.

Ibargüengoitia, Jorge. *Las muertas.* Mexico: Joaquín Mortiz, 1989. Translated into English by Asa Zatz under the title *The Dead Girls.* (New York: Avon Books, 1983).

————. *Autopsias rápidas.* Selected by Guillermo Sheridan. Mexico: Editorial Vuelta, 1988. "Agatha Christie: An Unlikely Obituary" and "Homage to James Bond," translated by Fernanda Soicher, in *The Literary Review,* 38, no.1 (Fall 1994): 45–46, 98–99.

————. "Jorge Ibargüengoitia dice de sí mismo," *Vuelta,* no. 100 (March 1985): 52–53.

————. *Dos crímenes.* Mexico: Joaquín Mortiz, 1979: Translated into English by Asa Zatz under the title *Two Crimes.* Boston and New York: David R. Godine, 1984.

————. "En primera persona: Punto Final," *Vuelta,* no. 31 (June 1979): 24–25.

————. "Otras voces, otros teatros. La vida en México en tiempos de Novo," *Excélsior* (18 February 1974): 5.

————. "¿De qué viven los escritores?," *Revista de la Universidad de México,* 17, no. 4, XVII (December 1962): 14–17.

Iser, Wolfgang. *The Act of Reading: A Theory of Aesthetic Response.* Baltimore: Johns Hopkins University Press, 1979.

————. "The Implied Reader: Patterns of Communication," *Prose Fiction from Bunyan to Beckett*. Baltimore: Johns Hopkins University Press, 1974.

Jauss, Hans Robert. *Aesthetic Experience and Literary Hermeneutics*. Translated by Michael Shaw. Introduced by Wlad Godzig. Minneapolis: University of Minnesota Press, 1982.

Jiménez de Báez, Yvette, with Diana Moran and Edith Negrón. *Ficción e historia: La narrativa de José Emilio Pacheco*. Mexico: El Colegio de México, 1979.

Keen, Maurice. *Chivalry*. New Haven: Yale University Press, 1984.

Kendell, Jonathan. *La Capital: The Biography of Mexico City*. New York: Random House, 1988.

Knight, Stephen. *Form & Ideology in Crime Fiction*. Bloomington: Indiana University Press, 1980.

La Cruz, Sor Juana Inés. *Neptuno alegórico*. Vol. 4, *Obras completas*. Mexico: Fondo de Cultura Económica, 1951.

Langford, Walter M. *The Mexican Novel Comes of Age*. Notre Dame, Indiana: University of Notre Dame Press, 1971.

Leal, Luis. *Historia del cuento hispanoamericano*. Mexico: Ediciones de Andrea, 1971.

Leñero, Vicente. *Los pasos de Jorge*. Mexico: Joaquín Mortiz, 1989.

————. *Asesinato: El doble crimen de los Flores Muñoz*. Mexico: Plaza & Janés, 5th ed., 1986.

————. *Los albañiles* (dramatic adaptation). Mexico: Joaquín Mortiz, 1970.

————. *El garabato*. Mexico: Joaquín Mortiz, 1984.

————. *Vivir del teatro*. Mexico: Contrapuntos, 1982.

————. *Estudio Q*. Mexico: Joaquín Mortiz, 1965.

————. *Los albañiles*. Barcelona: Seix-Barral, 2 ed., 1964.

Loubet Jr., Enrique, ed. "Ficción y realidad: Detectives," special issue of *Comunidad Conacyt*, 7 no. 121–22 (January–February 1981): 71-200.

Ludmer, Iris Josefina. "Vicente Leñero, *Los albañiles*. Lector y actor," *Nueva novela latinoamericana*. Edited by Jorge Lafforgue. Buenos Aires: Paidós, 1969.

Mandel, Ernest. *Delightful Murder: A Social History of the Crime Story*. Minneapolis: University of Minnesota Press, 1984.

Martínez de la Vega, Francisco. *Heriberto Jara: un hombre de la Revolución*. Mexico: Diálogo, 1964.

Martínez de la Vega, José, *Péter Pérez, detective de Peralvillo y anexas*. Prologue by Miguel Angel Ceballos, vignettes by Guerrero Edwards. Mexico: Talleres Gráficos de la Nación, 1952; 2 ed., Mexico: Joaquín Mortiz, 1993, Col. Narrativa Policiaca Mexicana.

————. *30 disparates sin prólogo . . . (Un libro de buen humor)*. Mexico: Talleres Gráficos de Excélsior, 1944.

Mendoza, Eduardo. *La verdad sobre el caso Savolta*. Barcelona: Seix-Barral, 1986.

Meyer, Jean. *Los Cristeros*. Mexico: El Colegio de México, 1977.

Millán, María del Carmen, ed. *Antología de cuentos mexicanos*. 2 vols., 6th ed. Mexico: Nueva Imagen, 1984.

Monsiváis, Carlos. *Amor perdido.* Mexico: Era, 1977.

————. "Ustedes que jamás han sido asesinados," *Revista de la Universidad de México,* 28, no. 7 (March 1973): 1–11,

Monterde, Francisco, ed. *18 novelas de "El Universal llustrado" (1922–1925).* Mexico: Instituto Nacional de Bellas Artes, Departamento de Literatura, 1969.

Mora, Juan Miguel de. *Desnudarse o morir.* Mexico: n.p., 1957.

Most, Glenn W. and William W. Stowe. *The Poetics of Murder: Detective Fiction & Literary Theory.* New York: Harcourt, Brace, Jovanovich, 1983.

Pacheco, José Emilio. *Las batallas en el desierto.* Mexico: Era, 1981. Translated into English by Katerine Silver under the title, *Battles in the Dessert and Other Stories.* New York: New Directions, 1987.

————. *Morirás lejos.* Mexico: Joaquín Mortiz, 1977.

Paz, Octavio. *México en la obra de Octavio Paz.* Vol. 2, "Generaciones y semblanzas. Escritores y letras en México." O. Paz and Luis Mario Schneider, eds. Mexico: Fondo de Cultura Económica, 1987.

————. *Posdata.* 13th ed. Mexico: Siglo XXI Editores, 1979.

————. *El laberinto de la soledad.* Mexico: Fondo de Cultura Económica, 2 rev. ed., 1970. Translated into English by Lysander Kemp under the title *The Labyrinth of Solitude: Life and Thought in Mexico.* New York: Grove, 1961.

————. *El arco y la lira.* Mexico: Fondo de Cultura Económica, 1956. Translated into English by Ruth L. C. Simms under the title *The Bow and the Lyre: The Poem, the Poetic Revelation, Poetry and History.* Austin: University of Texas Press, 1973.

Planells, Antonio. "El detective literario: Panorámica del género policiaco de Poe a Borges," *Escritura: Teoría y crítica literaria,* Caracas, Venezuela. Vol. 10, no. 19–20 (January–December 1985): 71–101.

Pitol, Sergio. *El desfile del amor.* Barcelona: Anagrama, 1984.

Poe, Edgar Allan. *Narraciones extraordinarias.* Prologue by María Elvira Bermúdez. Mexico: Series "Sepan cuantos . . . ," Editorial Porrúa, 1972.

Porter, Dennis. *The Pursuit of Crime. Art and Ideology in Detective Fiction.* New Haven and London: Yale University Press, 1981.

Preminger, Alex, ed. *Princeton Encyclopedia of Poetry and Poetics.* New Jersey: University of Princeton Press, 1974.

Ramírez, Santiago. *El mexicano: Psicología de sus motivaclones.* Mexico Editorial Pax-México, S.A., Asociación Psieoanalítica Mexicana. A.C., 1959.

Ramírez Heredia, Rafael: *Trampa de metal.* Mexico: Joaquín Mortiz, 1993, Col. Narrativa Policiaca Mexicana (Mexico, Diana, 1979).

————. *La jaula de Dios.* Mexico: Joaquín Mortiz, 1989.

————. *Muerte en la carretera.* Mexico: Joaquín Mortiz, 1986.

Ramos, Samuel. *El perfil del hombre y la cultura en México* (1934). Mexico: Espasa-Calpe, Col. Austral 1980. Translated by Peter Earl under the title *Profile of Man and Culture in Mexico.* Austin: University of Texas Press, 1957.

Revueltas, Eugenia. "La novela policial en México y en Cuba," *Cuadernos Americanos,* Nueva Epoca, 1, no. 1 (January–February 1987): 102–20.

Reyes, Alfonso. "Algo más sobre la novela detectivesca," vol. 21, *Obras Completas. Marginalia, Tercera serie: 1940–1959:* 412–17. Mexico: Fondo de Cultura Económica, 1989. Translated into English by Rebecca Lynn Feldman in *The Literary Review,* 38, no. 1 (Fall 1994): 62–65.

———. "Un gran policía de antaño," vol. 21, *Obras Completas. Marginalia, Tercera serie: 1940–1959:* 417–20. Mexico Fondo de Cultura Económica, 1989.

———. "Sobre la novela policial," vol. 9, *Obras Completas,* "Los trabajos y los días": 457–61. Mexico: Fondo de Cultura Económica, 1959.

Robles, Humberto E. "Aproximación a *Los albañiles,* de Vicente Leñero," *Revista Iberoamericana,* no. 73 (1970): 579–99.

Rodríguez Monegal, Emir. "Carnaval / Antropofagia / Parodia," *Revista Iberoamericana,* no. 108–9 (July–December 1979): 401–12.

Rother, Larry. "A Theatrical Scandal in Mexico," *The New York Times.* Arts and Leisure sec. (4 August 1988): 32.

Rufinelli, Jorge." ¿Quién es el culpable?," review of *El cuento policial mexicano,* de Vicente Francisco Torres. *Unomásuno,* literary supplement *Sábado* (12 March 1983): 11.

———. "Notas sobre la novela mexicana, 1975–1980," *Cuadernos de Marcha* (July–August 1981): 47–59.

Sábato, Ernesto. *Heterodoxia.* Barcelona: Seix-Barral, 1982.

Salgari, Emilio. *Capitán Tormenta.* Prologue by María Elvira Bermúdez. Mexico: Series "Sepan cuántos . . . ," Editorial Porrúa, 1982.

Sigüenza y Góngora, Carlos de. *Alboroto y motín de México del 8 de junio de 1692.* Mexico: Talleres Gráficos del Museo Nacional de Antropología, Historia y Etnografía, 1932.

Simpson, Amelia S. *Detective Fiction from Latin America.* Cranbury, New Jersey: Fairleigh Dickinson University Press, 1990.

Solana, Rafael. *El crimen de las tres bandas.* Vignettes by Angel Bracho. Mexico: Colección Lunes, 1945.

Sommers, Joseph. *After the Storm: Landmarks of the Modern Mexican Novel.* Albuquerque: University of New Mexico, 1968.

Spota, Luis. *Paraíso 25.* Mexico: Grijalbo, 1982.

Stavans, Ilan. "Divulgación de Rafael Bernal," *Excélsior,* literary supplement *El Búho,* no. 241 (22 April 1990): 5. Reprinted in *Prontuario.* Mexico: Joaquín Mortiz, 1992: 99–103.

———. "Sam Spade, Once Again (review of *Some Clouds,* by Paco Ignacio Taibo II)," *The Nation* 255, no. 6 (31 August–7 September 1992): 214–15.

———. "Xavier Villaurrutia y la novela policiaca mexicana," *Excélsior,* literary supplement *El Búho,* no. 374 (8 November 1992): 8.

———. "Olor a corrupción. Una conversación con Paco Ignacio Taibo II," *La Nueva España* (Oviedo, Spain), no. 131 (5 July 1991): 35–36. Reprinted in this volume as Appendix: Interview with Paco Ignacio Taibo II.

———. "An Appointment with Héctor Belascoarán Shayne, Mexican Private Eye (A Profile of Paco Ignacio Taibo II)," *Review: Latin American Literature and Arts* no. 42 (January–June 1990): 5–9.

———. "De regreso al *Ensayo de un crimen,*" *Revista Iberoamericana,* no. 151 (April–June 1990): 519–21. Reprinted in *Prontuario.* Mexico: Joaquín Mortiz, 1992: 25–29.

———. "Perfil del judío en *La cabeza de la hidra* de Carlos Fuentes," *La historia de la literatura iberoamericana.* Memorias del XXXVI Congreso del Instituto Internacional de Literatura Iberoamericana. Raquel Chang-Rodríguez and Graciella de Beer, eds. New Hampshire: Ediciones del Norte, 1989.

———. "Cervantes para Borges," *Anthropos*, no. 98–99 (1989): ix. Reprinted in *Manual del (im)perfecto reseñista*. Mexico: Universidad Autónoma Metropolitana, 1989.

———. "Detectives en Latinoamérica," *Revista de la Universidad de México*, vol. 42, no. 446 (March 1988): 9–11.

Steinbrunner, Chris, and Otto Pensler. *Encyclopedia of Mystery and Detection*. San Diego, Londres, New York: Harcourt, Brace, Jovanovich, 1984.

Symons, Julian. *Bloody Murder: From the Detective Story to the Crime Novel*. London: Penguin Books, 1985.

Szmetan, Ricardo. "*Los albañiles*, de Vicente Leñero, dentro de las novelas de detectives," *Confluencia. Revista Hispánica de Cultura y Literatura*, 4, no. 2 (Spring 1989): 67–71.

Taibo, Paco Ignacio. *De algún lugar a esta parte*. 2 vols. Mexico: Alianza Editorial Mexicana, 1990.

———. *Siempre Dolores*. Mexico: Planeta, 1984.

Taibo II, Paco Ignacio. *Algunas nubes*. Mexico, Joaquín Mortiz, 1993, Col. Narrativa Policiaca Mexicana (1st ed. Mexico. Leega, 1985). Translated into English by William I. Neuman under the title *Some Clouds*. New York: Viking, 1992.

———. *Regreso a la misma ciudad y bajo la lluvia*. Mexico: Planeta, 1989.

———. *Arcángeles. Cuatro historias no muy ortodoxas de revolucionarios*. Mexico: Alianza Editorial Mexicana, 1988.

———. *La batalla del Ché: Santa Clara*. Mexico: Planeta, 1988.

———. "La (otra) novela policiaca," *Los Cuadernos del Norte*, vol. 8, no. 41 (March–April 1987): 36–41.

———. *Sombra de la sombra*. Mexico: Planeta, 1986; translated into English by William I. Neuman under the title *Shadow of the Shadow*. New York: Viking, 1991.

———. *No habrá final feliz*. Mexico: Planeta, 1985; Translated into English by William I. Neuman under the title *No Happy Ending*. New York: Mysterious Press, 1993.

———, ed. *Bajando la frontera*. Mexico: Crónica General de México/Leega/Júcar, 1985.

———. *Cosa fácil*. Mexico: Grijalbo, 1977: Translated into English by William I. Neuman under the title *An Easy Thing*. New York: Viking, 1990.

———. *Días de combate*. Mexico: Grijalbo, 1976.

Thomson, Clive. "Problèmes théoretiques de la parodie," *Etudes Litteraires*, 19, no. 1 (Spring-Summer 1986): 13–19.

Todorov, Tzvetan. "The Typology of Detective Fiction," *The Poetics of Prose*. New York: Cornell University Press, 1977.

Torres, Vicente Francisco, ed. *El cuento policial mexicano*. Mexico: Diógenes, 1982.

Usigli, Rodolfo. *Ensayo de un crimen*. Mexico: Joaquín Mortiz, 1993, Col. Narrativa Policiaca Mexicana (1st ed., Mexico, América, 1944).

———. *Teatro completo*. 3 vols. Mexico: Fondo de Cultura Económica, 1963.

Valadés, José C. *El socialismo libertario mexicano. Siglo, XIX*. Ed. Paco Ignacio Taibo II. Mexico: Universidad Autónoma de Sinaloa, 1984.

Verne, Jules. *Miguel Strogoff.* Prologue by María Elvira Bermúdez. Mexico: Series "Sepan cuántos . . . ," Editorial Porrúa, 1971.

Vidal, Hernán. *Literatura hispanoamericana e ideología liberal: Surgimiento y crisis (Un a problemática sobre la dependencia en torno a la narrativa del Boom).* Buenos Aires: Hispamérica, 1988.

Winks, Robin W., ed. *Detective Fiction: A Collection of Critical Essays.* Englewood Cliffs, New Jersey: Prentice Hall, 1980.

Yates, Donald A., ed. *Latin Blood: The Best Crime and Detective Stories of South America.* New York: Herder & Herder, 1972.

————, ed. *El cuento policial latinoamericano.* Mexico: Ediciones de Andrea, 1964.

————. "La novela policial en las Américas," *Temas culturales.* Buenos Aires: Servicio Cultural e Informativo de los Estados Unidos (1963): 3–13.

————. "The Mexican Detective Story," *Kentucky Foreign Language Review,* vol. 8, no. 1 (1961): 42–47.

————. "The Argentine Detective Story." Ph.D. diss. University of Michigan, 1961.

————. "The Spanish American Detective Story," *Modern Language Journal,* no. 22 (May 1956): 52–58.

Zapata, Luis. *El vampiro de l ʌColonia Roma.* Mexico: Grijalbo, 1979.

Index